LIFE ON MISSION

GOD'S PEOPLE FINDING GOD'S HEART FOR THE WORLD

BY TIM HARLOW

Life on Mission
God's People Finding God's Heart for the World

Copyright © 2014 Tim Harlow

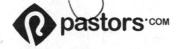

Published by Pastors.com
30021 Comercio
Rancho Santa Margarita, CA 92688

ISBN: 978-1-4228-0292-2

Printed and bound in the United States of America.

DEDICATION

To Denise, my partner in love and mission for 30 years. In my head and my theology, I don't believe God picks the perfect "one" for us to marry. But my heart tells me that either my theology is wrong—or I just got really lucky. I can't imagine **life** *or* **mission** *without you.*

The mission given to the church is both the most important and the most world-changing imperative in human history. **Life on Misson** helps to make it real and compelling for our day, in our world.

- **John Ortberg**, Menlo Park Presbyterian Church

Tim Harlow is deeply passionate about helping people find Christ. Discover how to connect with others, live a life of selfless service and develop intentional relationships that will have an eternal impact as you live **Life on Mission**.

- **Craig Groeschel**, Senior Pastor of LifeChurch.tv
Author of *Fight, Winning the Battles that Matter Most*

Tim Harlow helps us keep "the main thing, the main thing" in his powerful book and resource, **Life on Mission**. With crystal clarity Tim shows how we can discover God's mission for our life and live it out. If every follower of Jesus read this incredible book and embraced its message, our world would be profoundly impacted for God and for good.

- **Jud Wilhite**, Senior Pastor of Central Christian Church
Author of *The God of Yes*

We have a mission that really matters—for now and for eternity. Let my friend Tim encourage and equip you for the adventure of sharing Jesus with others. His book is an outstanding guide to a life of meaning and fulfillment.

- **Lee Strobel**, best-selling author of *The Case for Christ*
and *The Case for Faith*

Life on Mission couldn't have come at a better time! Tim Harlow's book lays out a clear plan of action for all of us who are willing to engage in changing our culture and helping lead people to an eternal future with God. I have accepted my mission and encourage you to read this book and do the same!

- **Alan Robertson,** Duck Commander

You don't have to know Tim Harlow long to know he is a man on a mission and has helped thousands be the same. A careful reading and resolute application of the principles shared will most certainly add you to the list of difference makers.

- **Randy Frazee**, Senior Minister of Oak Hills Church
Author of *Think, Act, Be like Jesus*

Tim has captured succinctly and clearly the principles of living on mission that he has lived personally, his family has practiced and the church he serves makes happen. Those principles are the very same that each of us are invited and called to live, regardless of our vocation or location. You will be challenged, encouraged and stretched as you read **Life on Mission**!

- **Rick Rusaw**, LifeBridge Christian Church
Author of *The Externally Focused Church*

Enthusiasm and passion leap off the pages of Life On Mission, as Tim Harlow challenges us to love the way God loves and show others the gospel for what it is: Good News. The combination of how-to with why-to, of solid biblical teaching with a generous dose of humor, keeps it real and keeps it relevant. Ready for a mission that matters? This is it.

- **Liz Curtis Higgs**, best-selling author of *Bad Girls of the Bible*

I believe this book will be transformational, because Tim Harlow is a transformational pastor who leads a transformational church. Tim issues a personal call to break out of safe-Christianity and truly live a life that marks others.

- Gene Appel, Senior Pastor of Eastside Christian Church

Finally, a book that steps through what it truly means to be a follower of Christ and helps you flesh that out on a daily basis. Tim's paradoxical style always hits its target. His humorous writing will help you become more serious about living a life on mission.

- Dave Stone, Pastor—Southeast Christian Church

This book is where ministry meets real life. Tim's writing is funny, sincere, and passionate as he teaches how to put the gospel on display and into words—no theology degree required. Ready or not, "qualified" or not, God's inviting you to be used in a huge way.

- Brian "Head" Welch, co-founder of the nu metal band Korn

If you want to live closer to the heart and actions of Jesus, you will love the practical, urgent (and funny!) guidance Tim Harlow provides. If you are part of the growing number of Christ-followers who are hungry for more than business as usual when it comes to how we live and what Church looks like, **Life on Mission** *is an answer, a guide-book, and a gift.*

- Ben Cachiaras, Mountain Christian Church

Too often over time the church drifts from its original purpose. In this book, Tim challenges us to return to the basic foundational principles that are essential to re-mission our church. This is a must read from a pastor who has grown his church consistently year after year by keeping it on mission.

- Don Wilson, Christ's Church of the Valley

Tim has lived what he's written about—his actions back up his words. And the evidence of it can be seen in the mission-minded children he's raised and the dynamic church he's led. Like Jesus, Tim lives his life with a passion for making more and better disciples.

- Jon Weece, Southland Christian Church

The reason **Life on Mission** *is such an important book is simply because it is a reflection of Tim Harlow's own "life on mission." Tim models life on mission, has led an amazing church to live life on mission and now, with this book, leads us all to live life on mission.*

- Greg Nettle, President—Stadia Global Church Planting

If I had a friend living apart from God, who needed to meet Jesus through his Church, who was willing to give a church only one shot—I would want him to encounter Tim Harlow and Parkview. Tim loves the mission and loves the people it's meant for.

- Eddie Lowen, West Side Christian Church

Tim Harlow is a leader who knows how to identify a mission and then accomplish it! In his book, **Life On Mission,** *Tim gives you the practical tools needed so that you can fulfill the mission God has for you by connecting, serving, sharing, growing and praying. God has a purpose for your life and* **Life On Mission** *will make sure you get it done!*

- Dave Ferguson, Community Christian Church
Author of *Exponential*

TABLE OF CONTENTS

FOREWORD

We were sitting in an open air café in Rwanda, East Africa, when Tim Harlow first told me about his passion to write this important book. For years, Tim has been a dear friend, a fellow purpose-driven minister and pastor of the influential Parkview Christian Church. Under his care, that wonderful congregation has grown to over 8,000 worshippers gathering in multiple campuses around the south suburbs of Chicago. Tim was assisting me in encouraging the over 4,000 pastors of Rwanda who've completed the first three years of training in the PEACE plan, and are now transforming that nation in amazing ways. As we talked, Tim shared his heart for reawakening the church in America for the fulfillment of the Great Commission. I told him, "You write the book, and I'll write the foreword!" You are now reading the fruit of that conversation.

This book is a vital book for a critical time. In a day when many churches have lost the vision of the Great Commission and their passion for bringing people to Christ, Tim has written a clear call to all Christians and churches to rediscover God's heartbeat for the world.

God has been on a mission since the beginning of time. From Genesis to Revelation we find God's plan to build a family for eternity, bring his lost children home, reconcile us to himself, and then send us out to share the Good News with those he sent Jesus to die for. Jesus made it very clear that the ultimate fulfillment of God's mission will happen eventually. The only question is whether or not our generation will get to be a part of the big ending.

Jesus said, *"This Good News about God's kingdom WILL be preached in ALL the world, to EVERY nation, and THEN the end will come"* (Luke 9:62 LB). Jesus also said, *"It is not for you to know the times or dates the Father has set by his own authority. But you will receive power when the Holy Spirit comes on you; and you will be my witnesses in Jerusalem, and in all Judea and Samaria, and to the ends of the earth"* (Acts 1:7-8 NIV).

The bottom line is this: If you call yourself a disciple of Jesus, **you were made for a mission!** God is calling you to join him in his mission in the world. No matter what kind of background and experiences you've had, God has planned to use it to reach others for Jesus' sake. You cannot be all God intends for you to be until you accept your life mission.

All of us want our lives to count. We want our lives to have significance. But, where does significance come from? Not from status. Not from success. Not from salary. Significance comes from service! Jesus said, *"If you insist on saving your life, you will lose it. Only those who throw away their lives for my sake and for the sake of the Good News will ever know what it means to really live"* (Mark 8:35 LB). This book will show you how to join God in the most significant mission in history. You will never find a more fulfilling pursuit than giving your time, talent, and treasure to being on mission with God.

Now let me say a word to pastors: For the fulfillment of God's Great Commission to happen, it will require more than just restoring the New Testament message of Jesus. We must also return to the methods Jesus used and modeled for us in his ministry. Through a close study of the Gospels, we learn not only *what* Jesus did in his ministry, but also *how* he did it! In four passages of Scripture—Matthew 10, Mark 6, Luke 9, and Luke 10—Jesus gives fifteen specific instructions to the mission teams he sent out. Unfortunately today, I don't know of a single mission strategy that is based on taking these fifteen instructions seriously. We just skip over them or explain them away due to our lack of faith.

That's why—ten years ago—I believe God led me to rediscover the Jesus model of missions, and we launched The P.E.A.C.E.

Plan, built on five mission activities that Jesus modeled, and fifteen specific instructions that Jesus commanded his teams to follow when he sent them out. The P.E.A.C.E. Plan is simply a return to doing what Jesus did, in the way he commanded that it be done!

Has Jesus' method proven effective? Yes! As the Pastor of Saddleback Church, I've watched our members catch the biblical vision of living "on mission." Today 24,869 of our members have traveled to 197 nations to serve other local churches through the purpose-driven P.E.A.C.E. Plan. I've seen firsthand, how this transformed our own congregation and also how it has blessed, reawakened, and reenergized every other church that has dared to go on mission with God.

Whether you travel the world to share Jesus, or you never venture beyond the boundaries of your home county, this guidebook can help you take your first steps in faith. An accompanying video curriculum is also available, as well as additional information and help from www.lifeonmission.com.

I want to encourage you to read this book slowly, with a pen ready to underline and a journal in which to take notes as God uses these pages to speak to your heart and call you to a life of significance. Gather with other friends to study it. Give it away to anyone who has yet to experience the joy of being on mission.

My father was a pastor for more than five decades, serving mostly rural and small town churches in his ministry. But leading smaller churches didn't mean he had a small mission. One of his favorite things to do was to lead mission teams to various places around the world to help churches construct their buildings. By the time his ministry ended, he had led more than 150 building projects for churches around the world. But his efforts were never really about the physical facilities. My dad was driven by the larger mission of finding the next lost person and bringing them to Jesus.

Just two days before cancer took my father's life, he was resting in bed, very weak from chemotherapy and radiation treatment. Suddenly my frail father began to try to get out of bed. Frustrated by his weakness, my wife, Kay, began asking him what he needed, how we could help him, and why he wanted to get out of bed. My dad replied, "Got to save one more for Jesus! I've got to reach one more for Jesus!" He repeated that phrase over and over, maybe 125 times. In the final moments of his life, my father was declaring, for one last time, the life mission that he had lived for. That day, with tears streaming down my face, I decided to adopt that phrase, "One More For Jesus!" as my own life mission. I cannot think of any greater goal for life. May God bless you!

Rick Warren
Author, *The Purpose Driven Life & Church*
Pastor, Saddleback Church, Lake Forest, CA
PastorRickWarren on Facebook

INTRODUCTION

THE TWO MOST IMPORTANT DAYS OF YOUR LIFE ARE THE DAY YOU ARE BORN AND THE DAY YOU FIND OUT WHY.

- MARK TWAIN

"Your mission . . . should you choose to accept it."

Every kid growing up in my generation longed to hear those words from the television series, "Mission Impossible." The agency would send a super secret tape player to the secret agent, who would listen to instructions (usually involving a dangerous trek to some communist country), and then the tape would self-destruct so no one else could ever know what the super secret mission was.

Interestingly, there was never an episode where the agent said, "I'm not feeling it, I think I'll go get a beef sandwich."

The assumption here is that if you are an agent, it's your job to take the mission. If you want to sit around all day and play Angry Birds®, you can work somewhere else. Maybe the DMV. But if you're an agent—you accept the mission. That's the whole reason you took all those Kung Fu lessons.

Guess what? YOU'RE AN AGENT. You have a mission. I don't want to spoil it for you, because it's not quite time for the book to self-destruct, but trust me on this; you have a greater purpose than beef sandwiches and Angry Birds®.

Over the course of this book we are going to talk through what it means to live a "Life on Mission." And this mission is not merely a matter of life-or-death. This mission is about eternity.

The mission is broken down into five actions. Let me say up front, this is not a "5-step program to reach your neighbor" (you won't find any tear-out tracts in the pages). It may be that you will find one person in your life and walk through all five of these stages with him. But that's not the point. These actions may not happen with one person, and they may not happen in this particular order. These are the actions we really ought to be doing all the time! Jesus is our example here—we're modeling our own ministry after his.

There's an urgency behind the mission. We've got to feel the gravity of the situation, to see the need around us—once we do, we'll be compelled to act. So we'll examine Jesus' instructions, talk about our circles of influence, and look at some stats that will hopefully help kick us into gear.

Then we'll head into the five actions that constitute our mission agenda.

"Connect" is about the fact that Jesus was always hanging out with the people *for whom he was on mission*. Most of us hang out in our churches and groups and are afraid of the very people Jesus would have befriended—the people right next door, or down the street, or in the next cubicle. We, like Jesus, need to be intentional about trying to connect with those who likely won't set foot into our churches. The good news is that it should be natural and may involve delicious food, depending on your proximity to good pizza.

"Serve" can be summed up in the oft-quoted Theodore Roosevelt adage, "nobody cares how much you know until they know how much you care." This is *not* about a gimmick to trick people into thinking that you care about them so you can sell them something (does that ever really work?). If you care deeply about someone, you will be willing to be interrupted and inconvenienced in order to meet a need, and this will help make God's Kingdom visible to others. Serving is proof of a gospel-consumed heart. It was crucial to Jesus' ministry and should be to ours.

"Share" is the part of our mission where things start to feel tricky. It shouldn't. Sharing our faith is not a matter of having pat answers or scriptures for every objection someone raises. I'm going to guess that for the most part, if we have mastered steps one and two of our mission, there won't be many objections to us sharing our own experience. And if there are challenging questions, you have full permission to say, "I don't know." There is a famous phrase (inaccurately attributed to St. Francis) that says, "Preach the gospel at all times. If necessary, use words." Well, IT'S NECESSARY. If Jesus is the only name under heaven by which we might be saved, we're going to have to actually say it out loud.

"Grow" may seem a little out of place in relation to our mission, but nothing could be further from the truth. There is a huge "discipleship" movement afloat today, and it's sorely needed. We are a generation of shallow Christians. What does that have to do with mission? Well, the command of Jesus was to "go into the world and make disciples." This means we not only help them find Jesus, we help them grow in Jesus. Any program that attempts to get people to step across the line of faith in Christ without helping them become disciples is missing the second half of the beauty of the Kingdom of Heaven.

JESUS SAID THE KINGDOM IS NOW. OUR JOB IS NOT SIMPLY TO GET PEOPLE INTO THE ETERNAL KINGDOM AFTER THEY DIE.

It is to help them see that Heaven has come to earth and we can have the Holy Spirit in our lives to help us every day. So we must not leave the newborn Christian babies in the pediatric ward and walk away. If we really care about them, and they aren't just a "project," then we need to help them learn to walk and learn to talk. Help them grow.

And here is the beauty of this awesome plan Jesus set in motion. They say that you never learn faster than when you teach. I say you never grow faster in your faith than when you're helping someone else grow in his. When friends ask the tough questions, you'll have to go find answers. Don't leave it to the Internet or your pastor. It's your job to "make disciples" and "teach them everything he commanded us." Then those you have discipled go out and do the same, and the mission continues.

"Pray." Jesus told us to pray for the Lord of the Harvest to send workers into the field. I find that fascinating since he was TALKING TO THE WORKERS. Why didn't he tell them to just… go work? It's the same reason he told the early church to "be my witnesses in Jerusalem—but WAIT FOR THE HOLY SPIRIT before you go." If this mission depends on me, we're in trouble. And that's true of you too, I'd guess. With God all things are possible. Without God, my best effort won't make a difference.

And there is a second part to Pray. The vast majority of the people around us believe in God—or at least say they do. One of the easiest things we can do to build a bridge to our friends is to ask them what they'd like us to pray for. We can be the friends in Mark 2 who lowered their paralytic friend down through the roof to meet Jesus, in a spiritual sense. People who would never accept an invite to church are surprisingly open to prayer.

If you are one of the people who has read the bestselling non-fiction book *The Purpose Driven Life*, you may notice that the five actions in our mission actually line up with the five purposes. This was, surprisingly, unintentional. I guess if something is right, it's just right.

Connect = Fellowship
Serve = Service
Share = Evangelism
Grow = Discipleship
Pray = Worship

This makes a great deal of sense. Your purpose and your mission should be aligned if you were actually created by God for a reason.

The agency is hiring, but you don't need an interview. You were uniquely shaped for this mission. Like a son or daughter groomed to take over the family company, God has hard-wired you to do this mission and to be fulfilled by it. You're the best person for the job.

For we are God's handiwork, created in Christ Jesus to do good works (MISSION), which God prepared in advance for us to do (Ephesians 2:10 NIV).

Here's how my buddy Rick Rusaw, Pastor of LifeBridge Christian Church in Colorado, put it recently:

> *I didn't grow up in a church, so I came to discover grace through some people that lived in our neighborhood who were just good people. I'm grateful for that grace. It changed the trajectory of my life in so many ways. We all love this idea that God does something for us. He gives us this gift. We love Ephesians 2:8-9. It tells us, "By*

grace we've been saved," and we didn't do it ourselves. We are so grateful. Can't buy it, didn't earn it, don't deserve it. He gives it to us, we accept it.

But we sometimes forget Verse 10, which, to me, seems to be the lynch pin of what God is saying to you. "You are God's workmanship, created for something He's already prepared in advance for you to do." This is part of the deal, that you are saved from something for something. We're saved from our sin, our guilt, all those little-t truths we live with, for something, not just to sit around, not just to sit in our small group, pass chips and coffee around. God has something He's prepared in advance for you to do.[1]

William Arnot, a nineteenth century Scottish pastor, put the matter this way: "To every true Christian these two things may be said: You have need of Christ and Christ has need of you." He then adds this thought: "The simple fact that a Christian is on earth and not in heaven, is proof that there is something for him here to do."[2]

This is what you were made for—and don't worry, God's already given you everything you need.

This is "your mission… should you choose to accept it."

OVERVIEW

CHAPTER 1

YOUR JERUSALEM

"I WANT YOU TO BE CONCERNED ABOUT YOUR NEXT DOOR NEIGHBOR. DO YOU KNOW YOUR NEXT DOOR NEIGHBOR?"

- MOTHER TERESA

"You will be my witnesses in Jerusalem, and in all Judea and Samaria, and to the ends of the earth" (Acts 1:8 NIV).

Put your mosquito net away. No need to buy Columbia zip-off pants that transition into shorts, or those $80 sandals, or water bottles that supposedly transform contaminated water into something drinkable.

You are not going across the world, across the country or even across town.

This is a mission to your Jerusalem.

Your neighborhood, your local bar, your gym, your supermarket, your office, your school, your home . . . your Jerusalem.

It may not sound very exotic or adventurous. You probably won't return from this mission with olivewood salad tongs that you can brag about at your next dinner party. In fact, if I do my job right, you won't return from this mission at all . . . ever.

Exotic? Perhaps not. Urgent? Risky? Life-or-death important? *Hell (-or-Heaven), yes!*

Before you write me off as one of those guys writing to only the "really spiritual" believers (and decide to go eat a beef sandwich), please hear me out.

When Jesus was asked to define the greatest commandment, he replied, *"'Love the Lord your God with all your heart and with all your soul and with all your mind'"* (Matthew 22:37 NIV). This was pretty obvious to his audience and should be obvious to us. But he didn't stop there.

"And the second is like it: 'Love your neighbor as yourself.' On these two commandments hang all the law and the prophets" (Matthew 22:38-39 NIV).

In other words, everything you need to know about following God can be summed up in these two ideas. Love Dad, and take care of his kids. And by the way, his kids happen to live next door. So at the end of the day, EVERY child of God is responsible for the well being of his brothers and sisters in the world. Obviously that has far-reaching implications which we'll explore later, but at its simplest level, this means that if our brothers and sisters who live next door do not know how to get home, we have to help them.

I know what you're thinking. "You're a pastor, Tim. I'm not. You've been trained and ordained to do mission work." Do you know what that means? That means I get a special parking spot at the hospital. That's all. I get it—you think this mission is my job. I work in Chicago, which is full of awesome, loud, sausage-and-mostaccioli-eating, multi-generational Catholic families. I love working with them so much. However, they (like possibly you) are used to a very clear distinct difference between the role of the clergy—and everyone else. The dudes with collars are the people who work for Jesus. They administer the sacraments, do the weddings and funerals, preach the homilies, etc. Most of the members are just along for the ride.

They call me Father Tim a lot and tell me that "Mass" was great today. So I have to spend a lot of time helping them see that we belong to a "Priesthood of all Believers" (1 Peter 2). I happen to be a guy who is paid to do ministry full-time, but we all do ministry. It's imperative that everyone in the church understands that they are clergy, too. (Just don't try parking in my spot at the hospital.)

The Apostle Paul tells us that there are some who have the gifts of church leadership (i.e. pastors) but that their job is not to do the works of service, it's *to equip God's people for works of service, so that the body of Christ may be built up* (Ephesians 4:12 NIV).

I know you may not be formally educated in theology; as far as I'm concerned that's probably just as well. What you have is influence. Who is better positioned to show love to your neighbors than YOU? Who has better opportunity to show kindness to your kids' teachers, or to pray for your co-workers, or to share with your personal trainer the greatest news ever to come down the pike to the human race? I may be better trained—but I don't know these people. You do.

Jesus left us with these parting words when he went back to heaven:

"You will be my witnesses in Jerusalem, and in all Judea and Samaria, and to the ends of the earth" (Acts 1:8 NIV).

"The ends of the earth" are full of excitement, as we've established. Other places in our own country—"Judea and Samaria"—are impressive, too. Heck, I'd take just about anywhere in America over Chicago, come February. A lot of fantastic work for the Lord is going on all over the world, and we should definitely celebrate it. But Jesus gave us the charge to go to Jerusalem first.

I'm not knocking "ends of the earth" trips. Listen—as some of the wealthiest people in the world, we have a responsibility to spread that wealth around to places that need it, and it's fantastic that we're doing just that! The good news about Jesus is reaching the corners of the globe as we put our resources to work. But what does it say about us if people are coming home to God in Tanzania while our own neighbors don't know him?

"I hear Jerusalem bells a-ringing." Stats will back me up here, friends: your Jerusalem needs you. You can't afford to overlook what's right under your own nose.

RIGHT HERE IN AMERICA

America now makes up one of the largest mission fields in the world. 195 million people don't go to church. (If those people were a nation, it would be the fifth-largest country in the world!) The percentage of Americans who don't claim any kind of religious worldview has gone from only 15% in the 1950s to 60% in 2010.

I had a friend tweet recently that he was on a plane to Dallas with 50 kids from South Korea—on a mission trip. To Dallas? Isn't that the *buckle* of the Bible Belt?

Take just the number of churches in Chicago, which has decreased by 900 in the last 10 years. Apparently they make nice condominiums. If you live anywhere in the UK, your local historic church building is probably a nightclub. What does that say to you? It tells me that we need to start thinking of our home turf as a mission field. Jesus said we start here.

This doesn't mean that the people in Indonesia are less important than the people in Indiana. It just means that the church is missing its easiest target. It's so obvious! It's like a baseball team without good pitching. (Sorry, there will be multiple Cubs references in this book.)

Jerusalem is the place you have to start. We're simply talking about the people who live next door. We don't have to get on a plane. In most cases, we don't even have to learn a new language.

So if 195 million people don't go to church, and the fastest growing religious group is those who believe in *nothing*, I think it's safe to say that we live in a mission field.

We just don't act like it.

For some reason, we've bought into a church culture of "sending" missionaries and waiting for them to report back to us at home base. If we're not careful, we run the very real risk of simply *paying* for mission elsewhere instead of *engaging* in mission right here. Clearly, we can't afford to do that anymore. We're losing ground at home.

At our church, we recently started a ministry to sex industry workers, thinking that this would be a great outreach in the Chicago area. When I announced it, we quickly found out we already had several strippers attending our church! Following our very first meeting, one of these young women left the church, went to her strip club, cleaned out her locker, returned to church the next day, and was baptized. That's pretty extreme, but the point is that she was already here! We didn't have to go to Samaria for this life change to happen. It happened in our own community.

REAP IT OR LOSE IT

A perfect example of this "witness" idea is the woman Jesus met at the well at midday. She was pretty far from being "Clergy." She had been married five times and was living with a man to whom she wasn't married. I don't know if this was her choice or she was a woman who had been dumped by the men in her life. Either way she was hardly qualified to be an evangelist. She had only just met Jesus, and from the tone of her questions it was pretty obvious that she had never been to seminary. And yet, she went back to her village and told the town to come and meet Jesus (read: she was a witness). The Bible tells us that the whole village came out to see him.

Many of the Samaritans from that town believed in him because of the woman's testimony (John 4:39 NIV).

That's the way it's supposed to be!

In the middle of this little "mission moment," Jesus asked, *"Don't you have a saying, 'It's still four months until harvest'? I tell you, open your eyes and look at the fields! They are ripe for harvest"* (John 4:35 NIV). Scholars say he may have been referring to the white turbans of the men of the town that were gleaming in the sun as they made their way to where he and his disciples were. Perhaps he was just being figurative, but either way, Jesus was deeply moved by the scene. The whole town was coming to hear him on the strength of one woman's story. *"Come see a man who told me everything I ever did. Could this be the Messiah?"* (John 4:29 NIV). One woman. One very simple story (just the simple story of what happened to her), and the whole town was affected.

Jesus said, "the harvest is ripe." That means the time to harvest is *now*! When the harvest is ripe, you either reap it or lose it.

I'm a small-scale gardener. I grow squash, tomatoes, and cucumbers. It's hard in the Chicago climate—tomatoes don't mature until September. You have a million of them for three weeks, and then they freeze. So you eat them, can them, freeze them, or they sit on the vine and rot.

When I lived in the south, you locked your car doors at church, not to keep people out—but to keep zucchini out. People were desperate to give it away.

When the harvest is ripe, you either reap it or lose it. And it's ripe now!

I ACTUALLY BELIEVE THE HARVEST IS MORE READY FOR REAPING THAN THE REAPERS ARE READY TO HARVEST.

The people of the world are more ready to receive the "Good News" than we are ready to give it. This needs to change.

I'm not one of those guys who likes to spend a lot of time decrying the post-Christian era in which we live. I realize that our nation was founded on biblical principles and that many of our founding fathers were Christians, and I'm grateful for that. But I think it's too late to "take back America." It's time to "take forward the Kingdom." The Church has always been more productive as a cultural outsider than an insider, anyway. Personally, I like living in a place where I'm needed. I like being a missionary 24/7.

But that means I have to think like one.

For our family, that kind of thinking has resulted in making purposeful decisions like not living in a parsonage, putting our kids into public school, working out at a local health club with non-church people, and having small groups with our neighbors in a neighborhood we've lived in now for 19 years.

The new word for this in church circles is "incarnational." Jesus was "God with us," and we are called to be "God with them."

The old word for this was "Christian."

As Greg Nettle says, "Jesus didn't commute to his ministry, he moved into the neighborhood."

To be honest, I'm not living incarnationally according to Jesus' definition, because Jesus didn't even have a house. Jesus' neighbors were the total outcasts from society. I can't pat myself on the back. But the least I can do is fully move in and take up my place in the community. Salt does no good in the shaker.

Luke 10:2 (NIV) tells us, *"The harvest is plentiful, but the workers are few. Ask the Lord of the harvest, therefore, to send out workers into his harvest field."*

It's great to ask the Lord to send workers. We should keep doing that. But we should also remember that each one of us is to be counted among those workers. So we shouldn't only ask the Lord to send—we should also ask Him to help us *be*. Fulfill our roles. We should be looking around every day and reaching out to those over the fences of our own backyards. Remember, we were made for this mission.

And honestly . . . if the fields were ripe for harvest then, what are they now?

The mission field is upon us. Jesus was so moved by what he saw when he looked out over those fields that he lost interest in the lunch the disciples had brought him from town. He said he had food to eat that they knew nothing about—the Kingdom, the Mission, was the driving force in Jesus' veins.

"My food," said Jesus, "is to do the will of him who sent me and to finish his work" (John 4:34 NIV).

I've tasted that food and it beats anything I've ever known. It's why we're here.

Step up to the table, people. The same dinner is being served up today right outside your door.

CHAPTER 2

BECCA ON THE BEACH

My daughter Becca was four when we lost her on a beach in North Carolina.

We'd been camping with extended family and having a great vacation. Becca was the youngest and was hanging out with several of her cousins. They had all gone back to the campsite over the dune, but Becca decided she would go back to the beach by herself and no one noticed. By the time we realized she was missing, she could have been anywhere. We immediately alerted the Lifeguards and started to search. My wife went north while I went south. When I say "went," it doesn't accurately describe my journey. I ran fast enough to qualify for the Olympics. I dropped off my flip-flops and settled down to that place in the sand usually populated by hardcore runners who know the sand is wet enough to be hard-packed for the best traction. I tried not to think about how it's also the place where children stand, dangerously unaware of the power of the ocean.

Ran? I *flew*.

I stopped occasionally to ask if anyone had seen a brown-haired 4-year-old girl in a blue swimming suit, and on I went. In a situation like that you don't feel like you are even breathing; I'm not sure your heart really beats. It's all adrenaline and sheer panic.

I was half a mile down the beach before I spotted her. I can remember the feeling like it was yesterday. If you've ever been in a similar position, you know that you immediately try to wipe the scared look off your face and act normal so that you don't transfer your own trauma on to your kids when you find them. So I was panting heavily, wanting to scream, and trying to be casual. "Hi Becca," I said, my voice bouncing around like an adolescent's. Becca's face lit up with an angelic smile, as if *I* had been lost and she had found *me*.

But then I had another problem. These were the days before everyone had a cell phone, and I knew that as anxious as I was in this situation, her mother was dying a slow death without the knowledge that Becca was safe. So I hoisted her up on my shoulders, ran almost as fast back up the beach to the place where the rest of the family was waiting, and then dropped off Becca so I could race even faster up the beach to find her mother. I couldn't let Denise live with the pain any longer.

Being lost is bad. Losing someone you love is worse. Becca, like a lot of people in the world today, didn't even know she was lost. She just assumed her parents were nearby like they always had been up until then. She had little cause for concern. Her parents, on the other hand, were basket cases. We knew better. We knew the dangers—all the awful things that could happen. Until we had her safely in our arms, we would not rest. Every parent is like that.

Even the Heavenly Father.

THE PURSUIT OF GOD

That's why his son, Jesus, was all about the lost. In Luke 15, Jesus was surrounded by tax collectors and sinners gathering together to hear Him speak, while the Pharisees and teachers of the law stood off to the side, muttering, *"This man welcomes sinners and eats with them."* This was a charge of which Jesus was actually proud, so much so that he proceeded to answer their accusation by telling three stories about seeking after lost things, and the joy of finding them—something the Pharisees would know little about. Their relationship was with the law and with maintaining their own religious image; his was a relationship with lost people like tax collectors and sinners who knew something was wrong.

God loves the lost. He sent His Son to seek and to save them.

THE GOSPEL IS NOT ABOUT MAKING PEOPLE RELIGIOUS—IT'S ABOUT FINDING THE LOST AND BRINGING THEM HOME.

One would have been enough, but he told three stories, each one about finding the lost. And Jesus described the lost as the sinners, the very ones the Pharisees were muttering about him hanging around. Actually sinners were very comfortable around Jesus, which is remarkable given that he was perfect and all. He was perfect, but he did not intimidate sinners. Probably because he loved them in their imperfection. The woman at the well had been divorced five times and was living with a man who wasn't her husband, Zacchaeus was a wee little cheat, the adulterous woman was caught in the act . . . and they all enjoyed being around Jesus because He did not condemn them.

So to illustrate His attitude toward sinners, Jesus told stories. The first one was about a shepherd who had a hundred sheep and one was lost. Given what we already know about the situation and the heart of God, it's no surprise that the shepherd in Jesus' story left the 99 in the open country and went after the one that was lost. And Jesus said he went after the lost one until he found it. There was no question whether he would find it or not. It's the will of the shepherd to accomplish what he set out to do and not rest until it's done. And when he found it, he threw it over his shoulder and came home celebrating, saying,

"'Rejoice with me, I have found my lost sheep.' I tell you that in the same way there will be more rejoicing in heaven over one sinner who repents than over ninety-nine righteous persons who do not need to repent" (Luke 15:6-7 NIV).

That last part was obviously for the Pharisees and teachers of the law who were probably thinking right then that they didn't need to repent, although nothing could be farther from the truth.

You can see why Jesus preferred hanging around the lost. They are so much easier to work with.

Story #2 is a simple one about a woman who lost a coin and turned her house upside down until she found it, but when she found it, she called her neighbors and friends over to help her celebrate. This story illustrates the fact that something might even be lost at home, maybe in your family.

"In the same way, I tell you," said Jesus, *"there is rejoicing in the presence of the angels of God over one sinner who repents."*

One sinner. One. We're not talking numbers here. We're talking relationships. It takes just one sinner being found to set off a July 4th fireworks show in heaven. One measly rotten sinner (like me).

Jesus spent his entire ministry with people who were standing on the outside of religion. He spent his entire ministry on the lost. He came to seek and save the lost.

To be sure, Jesus preached in the synagogue a few times, and he obviously discipled a small group of men (a group of losers when he found them), but his ministry was to the ex-cons, the tax collectors, the demon-possessed, the prostitutes, and the sinners. They were his target.

If Jesus hung out with the sinners instead of the self-righteous, it begs the question—why? I can think of two reasons: 1) they were more fun, and 2) though both groups were sinners—only one of them knew it. I guess those two go together. No one wants to be around spiritual pride.

We've got to climb inside of this for the sake of the world God loves. *For God did not send his Son into the world to condemn the world, but to save the world through him* (John 3:17 NIV). We've got to stop condemning the world and start loving sinners. Not just to "witness" to them but be around them, get to know them, and fall in love. Like God does. He's sending out messages all the time. He's sending out you and me.

The Reuben Donnelley Company in Chicago (at that time, the nation's largest printer of magazines) once had a glitch in the system and sent a rancher in Powder Bluff, Colorado, 9,734 notices that his subscription to *National Geographic* had expired. He sent in the money and wrote, "Send me the magazine, I GIVE UP!"[4]

That's God's intention for us. We are the messengers *and* the message. He's sending millions of us every day into the world. He's sending us to the lost until they give up, and they will give up when the message of love finally gets through. You are God's notice to the lost. You are God's ambassador (1 Corinthians 5).

The last story, the one about the prodigal son, is the best known of all three. It's like the theme song of our church. We like to think of ourselves as the First Church of the Prodigals. That's why we like to celebrate so much—someone is always coming home.

JOY TO THE WORLD

That's the one thing that brightens all three stories: the joy of the finding. The shepherd invited his friends and neighbors over to celebrate finding the lost sheep. The woman did the same when she found her lost coin. And the Father, whose son came home after squandering his inheritance on wild living, threw a party. *"For this son of mine was dead and is alive again; he was lost and is found." So they began to celebrate* (Luke 15:24 NIV).

We are assured in Scripture that even though there are over 7 billion people in the world, God cares about each one and knows each of us down to the hairs on our heads. God has the capacity to love more than one at a time. And he does not love Billy Graham any more than he loves you and me.

The Lord is not slow in keeping his promise, as some understand slowness. Instead he is patient with you, not wanting anyone to perish, but everyone to come to repentance (2 Peter 3:9 NIV).

It's as if Jesus was saying, I didn't make heaven for a few select people, I made it for everyone. I died for everyone. I WANT EVERYONE.

Do we know this? Do we believe this? Are we acting like it?

This is the heart of God. God is not willing for any to perish. And as long as there's one person on earth who doesn't know the Good News—one person lost—God says we've got to keep reaching out. When Jesus said, *"Go into all the world and preach the gospel to all creation"* (Mark 16:15 NIV), he wasn't just talking to pastors. He wasn't just talking to me. He was talking to all of us.

All these stories show us qualities of God's pursuit. The shepherd shows daring, the woman shows persistence, the father shows patience. All three are needed if we're going to care for the lost around us: courage to go into the world we would rather avoid, persistence to keep loving the unlovable, and patience to wait for hearts to change—or the prodigal to turn back—because only God can change a heart and He works on His own time.

LOST OR WRONG?
This may be the key to the issue for those of us living in the USA. We are living in a day of moral decline in the United States. It's a post-Christian era and Christians are having less and less to say about how things are decided in Washington. In reaction, some Christians have grabbed a soapbox to make sure everyone knows what should be right and wrong. Others think we can still legislate morality, and call for more action in politics. Still others just decide to stay to themselves and adopt an "ivory tower" mentality of retreat.

I'm not here to argue that we shouldn't exercise our right to vote or work to keep our nation or our state in line with the values on which our country was founded. I thank God for those values and the opportunity we've all had to live here for so long. But can we just get real? Toto, I don't think we're in Kansas anymore. If there ever was a "moral majority," it's a goner.

I don't think this is a bad thing.

Honestly, as you look at the history of Christianity you will see that it's always been most effective from the "outside." As a matter of fact, most historians will tell you that the worst thing that ever happened to the early church was when Constantine became a Christian and Jesus became "in."

Something Wayne Cordeiro said once really struck me. "Jesus never said we were the majority of the earth, he said we were the salt of the earth."[3]

Salt can't work unless it's applied *correctly* to something that needs it. Not enough salt is bland. Worse yet is the reaction to an overabundance of salt. Don't you remember in Junior High when some punk left the cap unscrewed on the saltshaker and waited in the distance to watch you dump it all over your chicken fried mystery meat? There is no recovery. Too much salt, together in one place, is at best useless and at worst disastrous.

I believe that is why the Holy Spirit allowed persecution to push the salty Jerusalem church out into the rest of the world after it was properly seasoned. Jesus wants us to spread out. He wants us to shine as lights in our communities, not to take over the light and power companies.

Besides—and this is the real point of this discussion—if morality is our main message, we soon become consumed with how wrong the world is, and before long, we don't even see people as lost anymore because we are so irritated by how wrong they are.

We need to go back to how Jesus sees the world. And remember, the "world" for him was the Jewish people who should have known better than to be lost! *When he saw the crowds, he had compassion on them, because they were harassed and helpless, like sheep without a shepherd* (Matthew 9:36 NIV).

Jesus never saw sinners as *wrong*. When Jesus mentioned to the Samaritan woman that he knew she'd been married five times, he didn't do it from an attitude of condescension. He knew that she was aware that living with a man outside of marriage was wrong, but he also understood the heartache that drove her into the situation. He knew the context.

He told the woman caught in the act of adultery that he didn't condemn her. They both knew she was *wrong*. Jesus never tried to convince sinners that they needed to go back and read their Bible again and figure out what's what.

Put yourself in the shoes of an unbeliever and think about how happy you would be to see a Christian coming at you who obviously thinks you are wrong and his whole purpose is to set you straight. The gospel will never get through.

Ben Cachiaras, the Senior Pastor at Mountain Christian Church in Maryland, told me that, "in a time when we are more needed than ever, the Church is pushing away the very ones who need the gospel, because of our refusal to be more interested in advancing the Kingdom of God than we are preserving America's moral foundation."

When someone is wrong, you set them straight; when someone is lost you go out and find them, and when you do, you embrace them and rejoice.

When Becca was lost that day on the beach, the last thing on my mind was to scold her or teach her a lesson about wandering away; all I wanted to do was scoop her up and hug her, and never let her go. Sure, I will teach her better when the time is right. But we don't teach first and rescue later. We rescue, then teach.

That's what Jesus did. *"Neither do I condemn you. Now go and leave your life of sin"* (John 8:11 NIV).

That's how the Father wants us to think about the world.

CHAPTER 3

H IS FOR HELL

THE GOSPEL IS ONLY GOOD NEWS IF IT GETS THERE IN TIME.

- CARL F. H. HENRY

There are 54 verses in the Bible about hell.

Oh, yes . . . we just went there.

We have to!

Jesus warned more about hell than he talked about heaven. That makes me as uncomfortable as it makes you. It's no wonder hell has fallen out of fashion as of late. Plenty of writers and preachers today are trying desperately to avoid the whole thing, and I understand why.

Once when my kids were little, we were trying to stay sane in a two-hour line waiting for 'Millennium Force,' the world's largest roller coaster at the time. Rachel, my oldest daughter, came up with a philosophical game to play: "Think of something the world would be better off without." (Honestly, I think she was thirty when she was born.) It was a bit deep for the amusement park, but it was better than my game of "try to maintain control of the railing."

So we used the alphabet and each person took a letter and decided something the world would be better without.

"A" . . . ants,
"B" . . . boy bands,
"C" was easy: cats, Cubs, Country music, etc.

When we got to "H" whoever's turn it was said, "Hell."

My sentiments, exactly. C.S. Lewis once said, "There is no doctrine which I would more willingly remove from Christianity than hell. If it lay in my power . . . I would pay any price to be able to say truthfully, 'All will be saved.'"[5]

Incidentally, God feels the same way. *"The Lord is not slow in keeping his promise, as some understand slowness. Instead he is patient with you, not wanting anyone to perish, but everyone to come to repentance"* (2 Peter 3:9). The hell he has set aside is not a place he wants anyone to have to go.

Well then, why? If God doesn't want anyone to go to hell, why have it in the first place, and why send anyone there?

One of my girls had a partial answer to that question that day at the amusement park. We were thinking the world would be better off without hell when she said, "No, that wouldn't work. What would we do with Satan?"

Questions like "Why is there evil in the world?" and "Why does Satan exist?" are some of the hardest questions Christians have to face, and we shouldn't speak flippantly, as though there are easy answers. I wonder about these things, as I'm sure you do.

But there is one important thing that the existence of evil in the world suggests to us. It shows that *we have a choice.*

God has created us with the integrity of a free will. We do not have to follow him. We do not have to do what he says. God wants a relationship with us, he pursues us, but he doesn't force obedience upon us. The tree in the Garden of Eden is still up for grabs, in a metaphorical sense—we can choose to believe God and be in relationship with him, or we can choose our own way.

It's not that complicated. In fact, singer-songwriter Bob Dylan put it pretty simply when he pointed out that we've gotta serve somebody; is it gonna be the devil or the Lord?

G.K. Chesterton writes: "Hell is God's great compliment to the reality of human freedom and the dignity of human choice. Without hell there is no choice, and without a choice heaven would not be heaven; heaven would be hell."[6]

Satan had a choice, and he chose hell. Every man and woman chooses. We either choose life with God or life without God. One is heaven, the other is hell, and you don't wait until you die to experience either one.

If we choose, that means we can't complain when we get what we want!

C.S. Lewis says that when it comes to eternity, we all get what we want—what we chose. "There are only two kinds of people in the end," he says, "those who say to God, 'Thy will be done,' and those to whom God says in the end, 'Thy will be done.' All that are in hell choose it."[7]

Okay, they might not choose that fiery place with the horned guy and his pitchfork—but people do choose to live without God. They either don't believe there is a God (an atheist) or they don't feel evidence is sufficient either way (an agnostic). And that, my friend, is hell—standing on the threshold of the greatest love known to mankind, and choosing not to go in. It starts with hell now, and it lands us there in the end.

The problem is that no one understands what life without God is like. Even the most cynical atheist gets to live in a world where God dwells. He can see and smell and feel the presence of God. There is love here—and God is love. People may not know it, but God is here.

"DISCIPLESHIP TO CHRIST IS THE GREATEST OPPORTUNITY AVAILABLE TO THE WORLD TODAY."[8]

-DALLAS WILLARD

James 1:17 says, *"Every good and perfect gift is from above."*

But at the same time, something else is happening behind the scenes. Something no one can see except as it is revealed in the word of God.

GOD IS HOLDING BACK
By the same word the present heavens and earth are reserved for fire, being kept for the day of judgment and destruction of the ungodly (2 Peter 3:7 NIV).

God is holding back his judgment so as to give more people an opportunity to respond to his gracious offer of salvation. It's like all those beautiful people out in California who wear Hawaiian shirts and flip flops, who surf and lie out in the sun without ever thinking that they are sitting on the fault line of a potentially disastrous earthquake that could put all that great ocean front property underwater in a few seconds. (They are smarter than those of us who live in tornado and blizzard land, but still . . .)

We all live oblivious to these inevitable disastrous consequences to sin in the world. The underlying fault line of humanity.

Hell is necessary. Like my daughter said, it's where Satan goes. But it's not where you have to go, nor do your friends and neighbors. No, the tragedy is not hell, *it's the fact that no one needs to go there because Christ died on the cross, and not everyone knows that!*

That's what we're here for: to let people know they don't have to go to hell. We're good news carriers in a bad news world. What we do with that good news has everything to do with our mission in life.

In Luke 16:19-28, Jesus told a story about a rich man and a beggar named Lazarus. As it turned out, Lazarus went to heaven and the rich man to hell. From hell, he was able to talk to Abraham in heaven and beg for mercy. Abraham told him that it was too late for him, and that's when the story gets interesting. The next thing the rich man could think to do was to figure out a way to warn his family about ending up in this horrible place. *"'Then I beg you, father, send Lazarus to my family, for I have five brothers. Let him warn them, so that they will not also come to this place of torment.'"*

The point of this story for us is the motivation for our mission. The point of this story for us is the five brothers who are still alive—five brothers who do not have to experience the rich man's fate if someone would just tell them about Jesus. Eternal life apart from God is so terrible that this man would have done anything to warn them.

Them? Our neighbors.

I'm not the type of preacher who thinks he sees all the signs pointing to the second coming, and has it all figured out. I still laugh thinking back to how convinced people were that Mikhail Gorbachev was the anti-Christ because he had that birthmark on his head.

I don't claim to know when it's going to happen, but I know that it is. I know that the mortality rate is 100% unless you are one of the *Walking Dead* (and I guess they are still dead).

I do know that 2000 years ago Jesus said, *"As long as it is day, we must do the works of him who sent me. Night is coming, when no one can work"* (John 9:4 NIV).

When was the last time you thought about the eternal destiny of the people around you?

I don't know if the story of Lazarus and the rich man is the inspiration for Charles Dickens or not, but God isn't going to send ghosts like Jacob Marley back from the dead to warn people. If you see the Ghost of Christmas Past, the first thing you should do is schedule a CT scan.

God doesn't need ghosts—he's got us. This is why we are still here.

This is why God doesn't take us home as soon as we become Christians. Though heaven is our home, God wants us to bring heaven to earth in the power of the message of salvation, that He might bring earth to heaven in the lives of those who hear and receive.

This is the importance of the doctrine of hell. It's not that we have to convince people that hell exists, and less still, that they may be going there. People don't respond well to threat. The street corner preacher yelling about hell might scare it out of some people, but most are going to look for a different route. But our knowledge of hell becomes a motivation for us to make sure everyone in our sphere of influence has a chance to respond to God's gracious offer of salvation through His Son, Jesus Christ.

What I'm talking about is a sense of urgency. Let me paraphrase a story from Bill Hybels:

> *I bring in the mail every night. When I come home from work, I stop at the mailbox, pick it up and go straight to the trash bin and throw away all the catalogs and all the junk mail. (I don't want my wife to get the catalogs.) I don't even bring it in the house. I just want to simplify my life. And then there are those appeals for charity. They usually go in the trash too.*
>
> *About once a month or so, I get one with a picture of lost kids that says, "Have you seen us?" A few months back, I was pitching one*

of these in the garbage when it fell down so that a picture of two lost kids were looking straight up at me. Suddenly I thought, "You just threw those kids away. Those are lost kids and you just threw them away. How could you do that in such a cavalier fashion?"

"Well, they're not my kids," was my first thought. "I can pitch it." And then my second thought was: "Good grief, if they were my kids, I'd be passing these things out by the fistful. I'd be looking for them night and day."

And then it hit him . . . The world is full of lost kids, lost teenagers, and lost adults, and they will be lost for eternity if we don't tell them about the good news of Jesus. God's heart aches for them, like mine did for Becca when she was lost at the beach. Abraham can't send a dead guy to tell them, but God can send us.

It's your mission in life, and you're the missionary.

CONNECT

CHAPTER 4

THE CHILI GOSPEL

Your mission is to eat. SCORE!

Seriously, have you ever noticed that some of our best stories and experiences involve food?

What would Thanksgiving be without turkey? Easter without ham? The Fourth of July without cookouts? Christmas without my wife's sugar cookies or my mom's strawberry pretzel salad (which is really just pie, but we call it salad so we can eat it with the meal and still have dessert later)?

And what would January be without grapefruit and cottage cheese and 8 glasses of water a day (and maybe a laxative if you're really desperate)?

I love food. We all love food, but there is something much more to eating than just filling up your stomach. It's not just the food we love; it's the experience of sharing a meal with someone. It's no fun having good food all by yourself.

Recently, I had to fly out on a Sunday afternoon to get to Bolivia. The window of time between the end of my last sermon and the flight from O'Hare was a little tight…so I had one of my law enforcement friends take me to the airport. Let's just say we got there a lot faster than I would have under normal circumstances. (If you haven't done 110mph down the Tri-State, you don't know what you're missing.)

In fact, I got there so fast I had time to sit down and eat. Instead of grabbing one of those hard cold sandwiches that have been sitting on the shelf since the Reagan administration, I ended up at the Macaroni Grill. It was a totally unexpected treat, but it didn't take long for the whole experience to sour regardless of how good the food was. I had no one to share it with. It was just me, surrounded by strangers. The food was good, but it wasn't a meal. I couldn't wait to get out of there.

So go eat with people. That's your mission. This is so easy, isn't it? But I'm not talking about eating with your family, or your church friends, or your small group, though that's important, too. This is about mission. I'm talking about moving outside of your comfort zone, like . . . wait for it . . . Jesus. (Here's a little cheat-sheet info for you—our model agent in "Life on Mission" is always going to be Jesus. That might simplify things for you.)

What I'm saying is that the reason I believe the average Christian has a hard time with Life on Mission is because they don't understand how simple it's supposed to be. We've come up with so many programs and strategies and formulas. Let's just start where Jesus did. If you never do anything more than connecting with your neighbors, we will be way ahead.

So go have dinner.

EATING WITH SINNERS
Meals in the time of Jesus were very personal things—you didn't invite just anybody to dinner. To have someone over for dinner meant that they had real worth to you. Usually, you had dinner with people like you, or maybe people who were a little better than you. It was an opportunity to be with your peers or to "play up."

Matthew 9 is the story of Jesus calling a corrupt tax collector to follow him, and then going to his house for dinner along with hookers, crooks, and all sorts of people that you wouldn't want to be seen with if you were playing the normal game of religion. You could get points taken off for eating a meal with people like this.

Tax collectors were the absolute lowest on the food chain among Jews for two basic reasons. First, they were swindlers. They would collect more tax than what was actually required and keep the extra for themselves. It was no secret that they got rich through this kind of deception. The second reason is far worse; tax collectors were employed by the Roman government. The Jews hated the Romans. They longed for freedom from

Rome. So tax collectors had sold out to the enemy and were getting rich off their own. Double bad.

And just like today, there were all kinds of taxes. There were bridge taxes, export taxes, import, fruit, wine, food, border taxes, and on and on. There was no rhyme or reason to the system. They would just set up these booths and collect taxes from the people to make sure that Rome was satisfied.

So here comes Jesus and His small band of followers and suddenly they get to a bridge or a border, and there's a tax booth with Matthew in it. Picture Monty Python and the Holy Grail if it helps.

As Jesus went on from there, he saw a man named Matthew sitting at the tax collector's booth. "Follow Me," he told him, and Matthew got up and followed him (Matthew 9:9 NIV).

Matthew, traitor of the Jews. Matthew, lowest of the low—so low he was separated from common sinners. There were sinners, and then there were tax collectors. The other disciples Jesus had already called must have been squirming. "Wait a minute," they were probably thinking, "we don't want that guy!"

Better pay attention to this. The last people you and I might imagine becoming Christians and joining our group might well be the first people Jesus is picking.

No surprise, when given the chance to follow Jesus—he accepted. Matthew got up and he followed Jesus. Notice there were no ultimatums, no requirements, and no rules of engagement. If we had been with Jesus, we would have expected him to say, "Okay, if you want to follow me—here's the deal. We don't drink, smoke, or chew, or go with girls who do."

But there is none of that, just a simple call to follow. It's the same invitation that has been extended to all of us, and is extended to us every single day of our lives. It's not an invitation to a religion; it's an invitation to a relationship. Follow me. Walk with me. Learn from me. Become like me.

Now there were some other people watching this whole thing, and they were very disturbed by what happened. How can you ask somebody this screwed up to follow you?

"Jesus, doesn't there need to be some outward evidence of holiness, or righteousness before someone can be called your disciple?"

No. The answer is an unequivocal NO. Why? Because it's not possible! On our own, there are none righteous on the earth and none who will be at any time in the future. Isaiah said our "righteousness" was no better than a filthy rag (Isaiah 64:6).

Please don't misunderstand me. We are called to holiness and righteousness. Matthew became holy and righteous. I'm certainly not encouraging you to become a sinner or "tax collector"—that would be foolish. It's the wide path that leads to destruction. I want you to get on the narrow path that leads to life. But this is the key . . . THERE ARE NO ENTRANCE REQUIREMENTS

You don't have to score at least 25 on your ACT to get in. You will *never* have your ACT together enough to follow Jesus. You will only be holy and righteous *after* you start following Jesus and have the Holy Spirit dwelling inside of you—not a moment sooner.

Larry Osborne pointed out in his book "Accidental Pharisee" that Joseph of Arimathea was *a disciple of Jesus, but secretly because he feared the Jewish leaders* (John 19:38 NIV).

Meaning, he wasn't a very strong disciple of Jesus, but he was one.

So now Matthew is on board and the stage is set for our next lesson, the means by which you and I are going to bring the kingdom of heaven to earth and earth to heaven. It's the essence of our message and the key to our mission.

They went to Matthew's house to eat!

That's it. That's the way we're going to change the world. We're going to eat . . . *with sinners.*

While Jesus was having dinner at Matthew's house, many tax collectors and sinners came and ate with him and his disciples (Matthew 9:10 NIV).

SINNERS WERE ALWAYS ATTRACTED TO JESUS. HE IS A SINNER MAGNET.

This was the greatest day of Matthew's life, at least up until that point. All at once he moves from being the shunned Jewish traitor to being invited to join up with the new popular Rabbi everyone is talking about. How is this possible? He, Matthew, whose only friends would have to be other tax collectors and sinners—scum of the earth in the eyes of the Jewish leaders—and suddenly he and his friends are in the company of . . . dare we say, the Messiah?

Jesus didn't seem rattled by the sinners. He almost seems to prefer them. He would rather be at Matthew's party than anywhere else in the universe right then.

In another passage (Luke 7:34 NIV), Jesus said, *"The Son of Man has come eating and drinking, and you say, 'Behold, a gluttonous man and a drunkard, a friend of tax collectors and sinners.'"* Why did he say that? Because he was proud of the association. He wore it like a trophy. He loves those of us who are sinners and he wanted the self-righteous Pharisees to know that. And besides, who wants to eat with Pharisees?

Actually Jesus did eat with the Pharisees on a few occasions and had a very different experience. In Luke 14, Jesus went to eat with Pharisees on the Sabbath, and a guy came in with a disease and Jesus healed him. Of course they got mad at Jesus for breaking a rule and healing on the Sabbath. Imagine that. They aren't happy for this guy who was healed; they are mad about the rules. And in another passage in Matthew where Jesus healed on the Sabbath, it says the Pharisees went outside and plotted about how they could kill Jesus. So you can't heal on the Sabbath, but you can plot a murder?

No wonder Jesus preferred the Matthew party.

Can you imagine the conversations that would have taken place? Matthew's house was filled with other people just like him. Most people had probably only heard a little bit about Jesus and what He stood for, but I imagine they could already see something different in Matthew. I picture Matthew running back and forth from the kitchen, making sure everyone was being looked after as he listened to the conversations that took place around the table and out on the deck of the house. Restocking the beer cooler. Music is pounding—you know Matty had a sick stereo with a kickin' subwoofer. It's non-Christian music on the stereo, of course. Matthew hadn't heard of "Mercy Me" yet. He didn't even know there were Christian radio stations.

I'm not just making light of it, folks. I want you to get a true picture of where Jesus was! It's only been a few hours since Matt was called. He hasn't had a chance to change anything about himself or his habits. He doesn't even know the code yet. He's just being himself. And Jesus loves him that way. If you're going to be in your mission field, you're going to fall in love with guys like Matthew just like Jesus did.

Many tax collectors and sinners came and ate with him and his disciples. That's the Bible's way of saying—Jesus was at a Naughty People Party! And when the Pharisees saw this, they asked the disciples, "Why is your teacher at the Naughty People Party?" *"Does your teacher eat with tax collectors and sinners?"* (Matthew 9:11 NIV).

This was so obviously offensive and morally incorrect that the Pharisees and scribes didn't even have to give any reason for their displeasure. He's not supposed to do this!

Why is it that he would publicly associate with them before they've made any changes in their lives? Jesus is doing everything backward.

Jesus responded to what his accusers said, and this is important. Verse 12: *On hearing this, Jesus said, "It is not the healthy who need a doctor, but the sick."*

JESUS WAS SAYING, "IF YOU THINK YOU CAN TAKE CARE OF THIS YOURSELF— KNOCK YOURSELF OUT. I HOPE THAT WORKS FOR YOU. BUT I'VE GOT THE ONLY MEDICINE THAT WORKS— IT'S CALLED GRACE."

Then he throws a dig at them, *"But go and learn what this means,"* and he quotes a prophecy they know: *"'I desire mercy, not sacrifice.' For I have not come to call the righteous, but sinners."*

Subtext: "I'm letting you know up front that my goal isn't to have holy little people that live in a little box and get everything right all the time. If that was what I wanted I would just take you all to heaven right now. But this is not heaven. This is earth. It's messy here, but we're finding sinners and getting them ready for heaven, and we do that by sitting down and eating with them, just as they are. Sick and messy. If you're good with that—pull up a chair and join me."

CHAPTER 5

MESSY LOVE

"MINISTRY IS MESSY, BECAUSE SIN IS MESSY. GET OVER IT, GET A MOP, AND START HELPING TO CLEAN IT UP!"

- PASTOR JUD WILHITE
CENTRAL CHRISTIAN CHURCH

We became friends at the health club and started working out together. He used loud, bad language, and not only gawked at, but also commented on every woman in the place. He's a huge, scary, biker-gang kind of a guy that you would walk on the other side of the street to avoid. And he was messy.

I've got to admit, it was fun to work out with him. Made me feel cool, and he pushed me. But he was messy. One day he decided to work out with me in a horrendously inappropriate T-shirt from a strip club. I tried to get him to turn it inside out, but to no avail.

It felt a little awkward to be honest. Most of the people at my health club know who I am—half of them go to my church— and here I am working out with a gnarly biker in a stripper T-shirt. It felt awkward until I remembered that I was supposed to look like Jesus—not a "respectable pastor." I remembered the Matthew party.

The ramifications of this for mission are extreme. I don't know about you, but until recently, I haven't had a lot of "sick" people in my life. I work for a church. I'm with staff and elders and Christians most of the time. That's my job. I'm more comfortable being surrounded by redeemed sinners, who know how to dress appropriately at the health club. Sure, I teach from the Great Commission, but I have to admit that lately it's felt a lot like *you people* need to go into all the world to make disciples. I can't go. I have to stay here and train you to do it.

Really? How can I be a disciple of Jesus without any real sinners as friends? I mean, it's what Jesus was known for, and he didn't get this reputation from going to just one party. This must have been a pattern. They said of him, *"'Here is a glutton and a drunkard, a friend of tax collectors and sinners.'"* (Matthew 11:18-19 NIV). Jesus never argued with them. Obviously he wasn't a drunkard or a glutton, but he never argued the "friend of sinners" part.

It's why the Son of Man came. This is who he is—what he's about. He is a friend of sinners. Plural. Maybe a few of them have strip club T-shirts.

And how about me? How about you? On how many hands can you count your non-believing friends? Not just acquaintances—friends. They have your cell number, not just your Facebook approval.

WE, THE SEEKERS

For too long now, we've been acting like our mission is to invite. Bring people into the four walls of our churches. We're more comfortable with this because everything is always on our terms. Invite them in. They're in our house now—they'll have to adjust to the way we do things.

But Jesus didn't say *invite*. He didn't say *bring*. He said GO. It's time for us to get used to being in their house. I'm so tired of churches full of people who are nursing each other along inside when we need to grow up and get outside. We've been waiting for "seekers" to come into our services, when we should be the ones out seeking. I hope your church is a place where people DO wander in and find Jesus; we definitely work hard to make sure that's the case at Parkview. But that doesn't let us off the hook personally. We are the seekers. Just like Jesus, who came to seek and save that which was lost (Luke 19:10).

We seek—*to build relationships*. This is of primary importance to your mission. Perhaps you are going to be called by God to be a street preacher—but I hope not. That's not likely your mission. Your mission is to your Jerusalem. The people right around you. THE PEOPLE WHO YOU KNOW!

So our mission starts with relationship. It has to start with relationship.

Let's think it through...

Picture a nice leisurely Memorial Day morning. You're outside replanting the flowers that froze over night because God never intended for us to live this far north. (Sorry, I'm venting.) Your family is hanging out in the yard, you've got steak on the grill, and suddenly up walk two way-overdressed people with a satchel full of papers and information. They are obviously from the Jehovah's Witnesses, or the Mormons, or some religious group you already know you don't want to talk with. What do you do?

I'll tell you what I do. If I have time—I mess with them, but that's just me. If I don't have time, I just tell them I'm a pastor and they move on.

But I'll tell you one thing that I never do. I never talk about personal and complicated spiritual matters with some stranger who just showed up at my door.

Do you?

So here is the question—if I, as a committed Christian who loves to talk about spiritual things, don't like to talk about them with strangers, why would I expect that anyone else would? They don't. I guarantee you.

I just had lunch with Dave Phillips, the President of the Children's Hunger Fund. He explained to me that they spent the first 8 years of their history providing food to be given by churches around the world. They were feeding a lot of children, and churches were being blessed to be a blessing to the people around them. But they didn't see life-change happen. Physical needs were met, but spiritual ones weren't. Even though they used the church for distribution, that's all it was. So that's when they changed their strategy to a home delivery approach. Now they give food, but they use trained people to visit these folks in their homes. It's about relationship—which is where real work gets done.

There used to be a Cheerios commercial where people would walk around telling strangers "I lowered my cholesterol!" It was clever, because they were obviously excited. But it was funny because *strangers don't care.*

I don't even care about your cholesterol level if I *do* know you, but if you're a stranger, forget it. That's why it's so important that we connect. We develop relationships with people.

MOST PEOPLE WHO COME TO A SAVING FAITH IN JESUS DO IT BECAUSE SOMEONE DEMONSTRATED CHRISTIANITY BEFORE THEY EVER DECLARED CHRISTIANITY.

I've never baptized anyone who said, "Yep, I saw one of those 'In Case of Rapture' bumper stickers, and I gave my life to Jesus right away, because I don't want to be around when there's no one driving that car!" I don't know anyone who ever said, "Yeah, I was watching Da Bears one day, and I saw a guy holding up one of those John 3:16 signs and I thought it was a phone number so I called it and the irritated person on the other line told me it was a Bible verse—so I went online, found that verse and accepted God's love right then and there."

There's this misconception that evangelism is about reaching people we don't know with persuasive speech. It's just not true. The crux of mission is relationship.

So we have some seeking to do.

If our primary mission field is our relationships, then we need to make sure we have some. This will mean taking the time out of our lives to interact more intentionally with some people we already know. It will mean being courageous. It will mean getting out of our comfort zones.

But if you were blind and now you can see . . . really, what other choice do you have?

A woman in our church sent me this email:

> *I had dinner at a restaurant on Saturday night and happened to be seated on the patio next to a continually growing group of middle-aged men and women. They were very loud and colorful as they enjoyed their round after round of drinks. My conservative friend and I had a hard time not staring at the interesting, rowdy group. At some random point in their expletive-laden conversation one guy at the table loudly asked three different people in turn, "So do you wanna go to the 11:00 mass at Parkview with us tomorrow?" (We have a lot of Catholics in this town.) I about died. He described Parkview as "refreshing." "Ya gotta try it with us."*

She wondered about the description of her church and the new clientele. But as she reminisced about it to me the next day she said, "I had to ask myself, if Jesus walked onto that patio, which group would he hang out with? Would he join my friend and I chatting about books and the psychology of men, or the rowdy colorful group?" She concluded, "I'm pretty sure we'd just get a polite wave as he pulled up a chair to the other table."

Brian Hunt is one of our pastors. He talks about one way to do it:

> *One of the places that I spend a lot of time is a local breakfast place. I love breakfast. The waitresses there have become a mission field—I'm just getting to know them. I am very proud to now have an omelet named after me. The PB (Pastor Brian) omelet is highly recommended.*

I've had a chance to talk with some of the waitresses there and get to know them and their families. One of them has started to come to our Saturday night service with her daughter. A lot of crazy family stuff going on there, but just through being able to sit around an omelet to get to know her a little bit and invite her to church, I see some transformation happening in her life. She is getting ready to go through a divorce, and I'm there talking through how we can keep fighting for marriage and keep fighting for those people in our lives that are tough to love, trying to help her know that God's with her. She's getting it. Who would have thought an omelet would have brought us together?

PIGS ON A BLANKET

This might require a paradigm shift. Jesus was usually found with people outside of his comfort zone, but even though the disciples saw his example, it took them awhile to get out of their own comfort zones with people after Jesus was gone. God had to shake Peter with a pretty extreme vision. An apparition of a pig on a blanket appeared that Peter was commanded to eat. (See, there is something about the food thing!) Jews weren't supposed to eat bacon, but God told him things had changed (Hallelujah). This vision coincided with a visitor, a Gentile visitor, which Peter quickly realized was the point of the pigs on the blanket. God was telling Peter, and all of us, to broaden our horizons and be ready to step out of our comfort zones—because everyone is welcome at the banquet table. Peter had a deep-rooted bias against Gentiles, but within twenty-four hours, he was ready to baptize them. And guess what? They were ready to be baptized.

We can't imagine how many people are all around us, desperately seeking a relationship with God.

"Surely no one can stand in the way of their being baptized with water. They have received the Holy Spirit just as we have" (Acts 10:47 NIV). This is a striking statement, coming from our devoutly Jewish Peter, but he can't deny the presence of the Holy Spirit in this roomful of Gentiles in Cornelius' house.

It took an angelic invitation to Cornelius to seek out Peter, and the appearance of the Lord through a vision to change his bias against Gentiles, but it takes him less than a day to be able to say, *"I now realize how true it is that God does not show favoritism, but accepts men from every nation who fear him and do what is right"* (Acts 10:34-35 NIV).

What a remarkable change! This was a pivotal event in taking the message beyond Judea to Samaria and the uttermost ends of the earth. The disciples suddenly saw the Gentiles around them with different eyes—their vision had to expand as the mission field expanded.

So does ours.

God is in the business of opening our eyes and our hearts to those whom we might have formerly thought were outside the realm of his grace and mercy. God wants us, just like Peter, to come to a place where we see every person as somebody for whom Christ died. You will find yourself loving people you never thought you could love.

We need to think about this every time we speak or react to those around us. We are in the presence of someone who God loves and values deeply. This doesn't mean we don't have conflict or that we don't have to confront one another or deal with sin in each other's lives, but it provides the context for all those interactions.

EVEN WHEN PEOPLE ARE AT THEIR WORST, THEY HAVE NOT LOST ONE OUNCE OF VALUE IN THEIR HEAVENLY FATHER'S EYES.

This is just as true of those close to us as it is of those far away. Your husband, child, boss, the teller at the bank, is someone God values deeply.

There has never been one person on this earth who did not matter to God. We need to get this perspective on our neighbors, our co-workers and the masses of people within which we constantly move. This kind of thinking needs to influence how we think of everyone, especially those who are different than us—different in ethnic background, politics, religion or economic status.

Jamie Snyder is a friend who used to preach in Florida and one day decided that God was calling him to reach out to a local abortion doctor. So he went to his office armed with a gift and a card for the doctor who also happened to be Muslim. He dropped it off with the receptionist and when she went back and gave it to the doctor he told her to invite Jamie back.

"What is it that you want from me?" the doctor asked.

Jamie smiled and said, "I serve at a local church and just wanted to bring you a gift and apologize for the way some Christians have treated you."

The doctor was stunned and said, "But you personally haven't treated me badly." There was a pause and then the doctor said, "You do know that I perform abortions?"

Jamie said, "Yes I do, and I couldn't disagree more with you on that. But I'm here because I'm genuinely sorry for the way some Christians have conveyed their disagreement with you."

Well, the doctor opened up to Jamie and began sharing story after story of attacks, vandalism and threats made against his life by Christians who opposed abortion. They talked for an hour and at the end of their conversation he let Jamie pray with him.

As Jamie was walking out of his office he stopped and said to the doctor, "When it comes to Christians you obviously know what we're against, but do you know what we're for?"

The doctor shook his head, "No," and asked, "What are you for?"

"We are for peace, patience, kindness, goodness, faithfulness, gentleness and love."

Mother Teresa said, "If you judge people, you have no time to love them." I've always found the opposite to be just as true—if you love someone, you have no time to judge them.

Honestly, folks, people don't have a problem with Jesus. They have a problem with Christians. Or I should say, they had a problem with Christians. Their bad experience may have been 20 years ago, but they probably had one. This is why it's so important that we not skip this first step and just be their friend. It's so hard for me because as soon as people ask me what I do for a living, I am tagged. There aren't very many pastors out there who aren't Christians (there are some). So it's hard for me to be a normal guy for long until they know that I'm a Christian. That's a disadvantage for me. It's not for you. You can be normal! Take the fish off the back of your car and just blend-in for awhile. Give them a chance to get to know you first. Be their friend, and do everything in your power to not fall into a theological/political/cultural discussion until you've earned the right to have an opinion.

Just love them. That's how Jesus did it.

CHAPTER 6

BARRIERS AND FISH FIGHTS

Let's talk about what not to do.

Did you know the Pharisees were evangelists, too?

"Woe to you, teachers of the law and Pharisees," Jesus once said to them. *"You hypocrites! You travel over land and sea to win a single convert, and when you have succeeded, you make him twice as much a son of hell as you are"* (Matthew 23:15 NIV).

That's pretty harsh language for the Son of God. Double sons of hell! The thing is, Jesus simply couldn't stand to have the truth misrepresented right in front of him. Nothing made him more upset than to see people representing his Father in heaven in a way that was inconsistent with the Father's true character.

The teachers of the law and the Pharisees were supposed to be God's representatives (at least that's what most Jewish people thought), so Jesus definitely had it out for them. Not that he didn't love them. He loves everyone made in his image, but he had to discredit their leadership in front of the people. He had to unmask their hypocrisy and correct their wrong teaching. Over and over in the Sermon on the Mount, Jesus says: "You have heard it said . . . (what the Pharisees taught), but I say to you . . . (what Jesus taught, the heart behind the law)." No wonder they didn't like him.

Jesus also said, *"Woe to you, teachers of the law and Pharisees, you hypocrites! You shut the door of the kingdom of heaven in people's faces. You yourselves do not enter, nor will you let those enter who are trying to"* (Matthew 23:13 NIV).

The Greek verb indicates that the people Jesus is referring to here are actually trying to get in! By promoting man-made traditions above God's truth, the Pharisees were literally closing the door on salvation. *"Woe to you experts in the law, because you have taken away the key to knowledge. You yourselves have not entered, and you have hindered those who were entering"* (Luke 11:52 NIV). No wonder he called them sons of hell. What they were teaching was keeping people out of heaven! So by Jesus' definition, a "son of hell" is someone who keeps people from hearing the Good News that can bring them home to heaven.

The same thing is happening today. The hell-boys are among us. In fact . . . I was one.

It can happen to any of us. The Pharisees were good people; they were the most righteous folks around, and they probably had good intentions. Still, they were keeping people from heaven and deserved the label Jesus gave. Let me give you my example.

SCIENCE VS. RELIGION

That's a pretty classic battle, right? Never mind that the two disciplines can happily coexist and even complement one another—we're contentious people, and we like to have an enemy. The issue of science and religion is not only debated in classrooms, universities, churches, and learned journals—it's battled out on the bumpers of cars. I call it Fish Fighting. Or Bumper Cars.

It began when Christians took the symbol that early followers of Christ used to identify themselves—the FISH—and put it on the bumpers of their cars. Hardly anybody knew what it meant. In the early church it was a way to quietly and safely identify a fellow believer. But it didn't stay silent for long. Someone got bolder and put the word IXTHUS inside the fish, which is a Greek acronym for Jesus, Christ, God's Son, and our Savior. But that was still pretty tame. Who speaks Greek, after all? Eventually some Christians displayed a fish symbol with the word "Jesus" inside, and that's when it started.

Some folks who weren't sympathetic to Christianity started chafing at the visibility of all these symbols, and so they thought of a comeback. They designed their own fish with Darwin's name inside, and four little legs and feet. It was their way of suggesting one of the main tenants of evolution, in which the fish evolved and walked out of the ocean.

Well, Christians can be sarcastic, too, and so believers retaliated with a two-fish design: it was the Darwinian evolution fish being eaten by a larger "Truth" fish. Brilliant. Well, then the evolution team fought back with a large dinosaur eating the truth fish. Thankfully at the time of this writing, there is no comeback from Creationists. Here we are in the enlightened twenty-first century, with people yelling at each other from the bumpers of their cars.

I wonder what God thinks?

I was a hell-boy with this one for a while. I studied science in high school and learned about the theory of evolution, just like everyone else. But I was in the Bible belt, so most of us just rolled our eyes and went along with it. We didn't really even touch the subject in my undergraduate work at Bible college. It was just assumed that "those people don't believe in God" and we pitied them because they couldn't deduce a Creator from his creation. But as I got further down the trail of education, I found out that there were some credible scientists who did not believe in Darwinian evolution. Up to this point, it felt like it was science vs. the Bible, and somehow in my simple mind it didn't matter, because God said it, I believed it, and that settled it.

However, now there was a whole discipline devoted to "Intelligent Design," and some of these people were respected scientists who actually believed in creation. Well, I've never been a very even-keeled sort of guy. So when I got wind of this new learning, I just went off on it. I wrote a paper for a class project called, "Creationism for My Child's Teacher." It was something designed to give to the teachers in the public school system where my girls attended. Every year at parent/teacher conferences, I would confer this document on all science teachers so that they would know that I was a Christian and my kids didn't believe their evolutionary blather.

I was careful to be kind and was usually kindly received at least on the surface. Soon, many in our congregation started taking copies and passing them around their schools and neighborhoods. I did hear from some people, third-hand, that some of my sources were not well researched and the facts were sketchy, but that didn't deter me. I also preached a series of sermons on the subject, and had some large attendance numbers and great reviews from the faithful.

All this time, there was a man in my congregation who had a PhD in psychology. He was fun to be around and someone I considered a friend. But as he began to develop in his faith, he started to get hung up on this issue. He had obviously studied a lot more science than anyone else I knew, and he could not totally buy creationism. He wasn't against a God who started it all, but he could not buy the whole young earth, creationist package. I also started to know more and more Christians who didn't agree with everything I'd been reading, like the debate between traditional young earth Christians, and those who believe in an old earth creationism (with regular scientific age-dating theories), and even theistic evolutionists (who believe God started the cell and let her rip). In other words, there wasn't even agreement among believers about the things I was teaching.

One day my smart friend asked me, "Do I have to believe in your views on creation to be a Christian?" And that's when I stopped and said (to myself) "son of hell."

After many years, God started working on my heart. Through several other encounters with atheists and unbelievers, I found that every time we'd try to have a conversation about anything spiritual, it seemed to always slide back into a creation/evolution debate and stopped there. Suddenly I realized that I was fighting a battle that was keeping me from winning the war. Does a person need to believe in seven literal days of creation to become a Christian? Do they need to believe that macroevolution is impossible in order to make it into heaven? The answer is an emphatic NO, and I began to realize I had been acting like a son of hell, keeping people from the kingdom because I thought I was defending the truth.

I don't think the Bible says "Believe on the name of the Lord Jesus—and in a six thousand year-old planet—and you will be saved." It's just not a salvation issue. I'm still confident that God created, that he created on *purpose*, and that creation was an act of love. Don't get me wrong. I just decided to not have an opinion on the age of the earth. Because most of the people I know who do, use it as a war cry instead of a motivator for acts of love.

Is someone's salvation tied into my understanding of a certain doctrinal stance on the beginning of the world? No. The end of the world? No. The gifts of the Spirit? No. Which party to vote for? No. Which baseball team to root for? No.

We're not going to get to the pearly gates and hear Peter ask, "Answer me these questions three, ere the other side you see! What is your name? What is your quest? What is the timeline of Genesis 1?"

If we are on a mission to connect with the world, the sons-of-hell battles need to be laid aside so that I don't alienate the very people he wants to reach through me.

The truth of the matter is that arguing with someone is never going to get them to know and love Jesus. Jesus never argued anyone into his kingdom. Catch this—the only people Jesus ever argued with were the *sons of hell*.

"WE NEVER WIN OUR ENEMIES TO CHRIST, ONLY OUR FRIENDS."

- RICK WARREN

I realized that I had stumbled on a whole host of barriers to the gospel that we have erected in the name of our own Christian causes instead of the name of Jesus.

I was buying into a corporate Christian agenda that was making enemies of the world for whom Christ died. I was making "sons of hell." When we Christians try to get everybody to agree with our version of what the world should look like, instead of allowing people to come to Jesus, just as they are, we are blocking them from a relationship with God.

Just listen to this quote from an atheist named Hemet Mehta. He spent some time going to different churches to try to understand Christianity— from the outside.

> As I read Christian books and spent months attending an amazing variety of churches in different parts of the country, I kept running across a consistent and troubling truth about American Christianity. It is clear that most churches have aligned themselves against non-religious people. And by adopting this stance, Christians have turned off the people I would think they would want to connect with. The combative stance I have observed in many churches and for many Christians on an individual level is an approach that has caused people to become apathetic, and even antagonistic towards religion as a whole. By displaying a negative attitude towards anyone

outside their community, people of faith make
enemies of those who don't believe the same God
they do."[9]

Does it take an atheist to show us the damage we are doing? It's time to lay down our banners and causes and pick up the banner of love. I don't know about you, but I don't want to get to heaven and have God say, "Harlow, why did you let your feeble brain and your self-proclaimed causes get in the way of my children coming home? How did you forget that was the reason you were there?"

A recent Barna Group research study showed that eighty-seven (87%) percent of the young people outside the church between the ages of 18 and 35 think the church is judgmental.[10] Eighty-seven percent! This doesn't mean all Christians are judgmental, but it's certainly a prevailing perception and it came from somewhere. It has some ground in fact. To some extent, we're all guilty of judgment. We're guilty of condemning. We're guilty of being sons of hell, keeping people we don't like or agree with out of heaven. I'm guilty of it, and maybe you are, too.

When people need a helping hand, they don't need a hand of judgment. They don't need a hand of accusation. They need a hand of love and grace.

Please remember Jesus' reaction when he was confronted with the opportunity to choose between a cause and a person. There was this woman who was caught in the act of adultery. *In the act.* I mean, they caught her in bed with the guy. And they brought her to Jesus. You can just imagine the Pharisees' delight! They didn't like Jesus. They didn't like being called sons of hell.

"What are we going to do with this woman?" they asked Jesus. "The law says we should stone her. What do you say we should do?" There was no way he could let her off—either he would defy the law of Moses, or he would have to align with the Pharisees. If he stones her, he's going to be on our side. So, we've got him.

Jesus' response is priceless. "You're absolutely right. We should stone her. So whichever one of you is without sin . . . be my guest." And you know the story; one by one they drop their rocks and leave. The Scripture says the older ones left first, down to the younger. Makes sense—the older, wiser ones know their sin better than the younger, arrogant idealists who haven't lived long enough to regret anything.

And Jesus turned to the woman, who is probably burning with shame and humiliation, and said, "Has no one condemned you?" She probably didn't even look up: "No one sir." Knowing that he actually could throw the rock—he actually was without sin—Jesus said instead, "Then neither do I condemn you. Go and leave your life of sin." The wall was down. Now she could have a relationship with God, and go live a new way of life.

I want to tell you something. No one is out of God's reach. God doesn't write off anyone, even though we do. And if Christians could understand this—churches would not be able to build enough buildings or add enough services. Because there are literally billions of people out there who are waiting for the wall to come down so that they can get home.

ROCK SOLID

My daughter Rachel spent five months in Birmingham, England, working with a campus ministry at the University of Birmingham. During that time, she developed a relationship with a brilliant student who was working on his Master's degree in computer security (i.e., trying to legitimize his hacking habit).

Ash was not at all interested in "Religion." He was the stereotypical English Millennial—a great heart, an amazing mind, and a skeptical, searching soul. He didn't need the trappings of organized religion and was quite adept at shooting down the silly blokes who would try to argue it with him. That was, until he came into contact with a ministry full of young Americans who were willing to *join him at the pub* and actually listen to his questions.

After she went back to her college to finish her degree, she and Ash stayed in contact with long discussions via Al Gore's Internet thingy.

Over time, he started to come around, and . . . well I'll let you in on one of their g-chat conversations.

> *Ash: When I met you, I could have (and had in the past) given you hours of justification for why I hated religion. I could have reeled off a list and put you, as a religious fanatic, in your place. Had you come at me and challenged why I hated religion, I would have told you why I pitied people who believed in God and Jesus and the resurrection. And, no offense, I would probably have come away looking pretty smug for all my excellent arguments and rational victories of logic.*
>
> *But you didn't, you just went ahead and showed me that it was all bull (well, he used a naughty word here) and that most of my facts are opinions wrapped in justification.*
>
> *Well, the best analogy I can think of is kinda biblical but I'm gonna risk it. It's like I spent years building all these foundations to stand on, and people would come and say, 'Hey, your foundations are looking pretty rubbish' and I'd throw stuff at them and tell 'em to bugger off—they were, after all, just standing in the mud.*
>
> *And then you (Rachel) showed up.*
>
> *And you walk up, and instead of pointing fun at my rubbish foundations, you just walk over and stand on a rock. I'm looking over thinking, hang on, she's not saying it but . . .*

that rock required no building at all, and it looks sturdier than my foundations. And you haven't got to tell me, 'cause I can see the damned rock.

No argument. No preaching. Just standing on a rock. The witness was Rachel being real.

Ash became a Christ-follower not because anyone argued him into the kingdom, but because someone was a witness. The word "witness" in the Scriptures is almost always a noun, not a verb. A witness is who you are, not something you do. "You will be my witnesses," Jesus said.

I know this story well, because over the course of those months, he became a Christian. Rachel actually flew back over to visit the team there and baptized him in a river in Wales. Then, in the almost Hallmark Channel storyline, he proceeded to hack his way into my daughter's heart and ultimately became my son-in-law and the father of my grandchildren. You can see why it is one of my favorite witnessing stories ever. I couldn't love him more (I'm still working on his language)!

If you're fortunate enough to be standing on the Rock, just remember that God didn't give it to you as a soapbox. It's not your preaching platform. You're on the Rock to put God's love, grace, and power on display, not to judge the people who might be standing in the mud. If others can see that kind of love and power in your life, who knows? When you reach your hand down to them, they might just be inclined to take it.

SERVE

CHAPTER 7

THE SKUNK DILEMMA

PEOPLE DON'T CARE HOW MUCH YOU KNOW
UNTIL THEY KNOW HOW MUCH YOU CARE.

- THEODORE ROOSEVELT

Connecting with someone is a great first step. It's the first thing Jesus did after Matthew joined his growing band of misfits and followers. But for Jesus and his disciples, those meals with tax collectors and sinners were the entry point to a three-year journey.

As you know by now, ground zero for our mission is the field of relationships, and as you get to know people, there will come a point when you need to prove they are your friends and not your "projects." That takes work. It's messy. It means being genuine and being vulnerable yourself to your own process. (You can't ask someone to be something you are unwilling to be.)

It starts where Jesus started, through being a servant. *"For even the Son of Man did not come to be served, but to serve, and to give his life as a ransom for many"* (Mark 10:45 NIV).

When you read the Bible and you read about Jesus, you read about how he always rooted for the underdog—the powerless, the poor, the left behind, the imprisoned, the orphaned, the widowed, the aged, the mentally ill, the social outcasts, the sick and the lepers— people Jesus called "the least of these," and he wants those people to be equally important to us. Who else is going to look after them if we don't? So many social programs have been left on the cutting room floor. There's not enough money in the system to shield these people or separate them from the rest of society. They are spilling into our streets. You don't have to go far to find them.

The least of these . . . who would you consider the least of these? Those who will never be able to pay you back? Those whose choices have put them in a difficult situation? Those of a different race? Those who came from a country which you disagree with politically? Those who belong to a different denomination or religion? Those whose sexual preference runs against the biblical model? I don't believe that we have permission to exclude anyone from our acts of compassion, because these were all people who Jesus came to serve.

Don't forget—Jesus didn't come for the healthy.

"It's not the healthy who need a doctor, but the sick" (Matthew 9:12 NIV).

On this broken planet, hardly any of us fit in that category anyway!

There is a line you have to cross by connecting with outsiders in the first place. But there is another line you cross when you move from eating to serving. Hanging out in a restaurant is a start, but it's not enough. The Bible says that on *that* day Jesus is going to separate people into two groups. To one, he'll say, *"I was hungry, and you fed me. I was thirsty and you gave me a drink. I was a stranger, and you invited me into your home. I was naked, and you gave me clothing. I was sick and you cared for me. I was in prison and you visited me."* And the people in this group will not get it. They will be surprised and ask, *"When did we do that for you, Lord?"* *"When you have done it to one of the least of my brothers or sisters, you've done it to me."*

The impression here is they were just doing what their heart told them to do. It wasn't any big deal to them—they were just serving as God would want them to do. They weren't earning their way to heaven, they weren't trying to gain brownie points, they weren't trying to be noticed, and they certainly weren't keeping some kind of moral score like the Pharisees did. They were just doing what they felt God wanted them to do, little knowing they were touching Jesus.

This should be exactly the same way your neighbors and friends see you. Our motivation for being servant-hearted people should be completely different than everyone else's. Christianity is really the only system in which you CANNOT earn heaven by good works. There is no karma. There is no enlightenment reserved for even the most disciplined followers. All good gifts (including our entry to heaven) are God's grace, and any good on our part is simply a natural response. We love because we have been loved.

So it's time to cross the line into deeper friendship. If you feel a little daunted, you aren't alone.

Elizabeth Sherrill is a writer and publisher from Chappaqua, New York. One day she was writing at her word processor, and she looked out the window and saw a skunk stumbling through her backyard with what looked like a yellow helmet attached to its head. Closer scrutiny revealed it wasn't a yellow helmet; it was a yogurt carton. The skunk had been trying to eat out of this yogurt carton, got it stuck on its head, and was now frantically trying to free itself.

Elizabeth, who was watching this whole scene unfold from her computer, said to herself, "Somebody should do something about that." And then she said to herself, "Somebody besides me should do something about that. Surely, someone will come along. Certainly at some point this skunk will make its way out of my yard and into someone else's." It didn't happen.

Eventually she realized she was the only person in a position to do something about the poor creature, so she called the city and talked to someone from Animal Control. "Listen. I've got a skunk in my backyard. He's wearing a yogurt carton. What should I do?"

The man said, "You need to remove the carton from its head."

And she said, "Well, what if this skunk sprays me? What do I do then?"

"Well, you're fine because if the skunk can't see you, he can't spray you."

"Yeah, but what about when I actually take it off?" There was this moment of silence on the phone, and the man said, "Well, do your best not to make the skunk feel threatened."

So she agreed to this and walked outside reluctantly only to find the skunk had disappeared. It wasn't anywhere to be found. And just when she thought she was off the hook, this black and white streak comes running towards her from the bushes. Without thinking of the implications, she reached down, grabbed hold of that yellow carton and pulled as hard as she could, and suddenly she came face to face with the skunk. She said she held its gaze for a full ten seconds trying not to make it feel threatened, and finally, the skunk turned around and ran off.

To this day, she calls this "a timeless parable" that played itself out in her backyard. "I realize now that the skunk was all those needs I hesitate to get involved in. Involvement takes time and I have deadlines to make. I probably can't do anything anyway. Somebody else can handle it better. Besides, involvement can be ugly and the stench may rub off on you. And all those things, of course, may be true," she wrote, "but I've got a yellow pencil holder on my desk, a rather scratched and battered one, to remind me that every now and then God answers a need with *me*."[11]

Let me take a moment to introduce you to the mission analogy of your home. It starts in your backyard. Mark Mittleberg calls this the "barbeque-first" principle in "Contagious Christian," the book he wrote with Bill Hybels. So for us, "Connect" is about inviting people into your backyard where it's safe for them. If they decide not to enter into a deeper relationship with you, there is an easy way out.

"Serve" is where we go to the next level—when we invite them inside. Even if it's just for a meal, there is something more personal about eating a meal inside than outside on the patio. And inside is where you can meet their needs. You can allow them to use the bathroom, give them a Band-Aid®, and even let them spend the night if there is a reason. Inside is where they become more like family. You meet the needs of your family.

It'll look different for everybody, but the truth remains: God wants to answer a need with you. You really can have feet like Jesus' feet that take you to where people are far from God, because they're everywhere, and you can have hands like Jesus' hands that touch the hurting and the unclean. They exist in the uttermost parts of the world, to be sure. I've been there. They will be in Samaria and Judea, too. We are responsible for all of them. But as important as child sponsorship and global missions programs are (and as much as I love these programs), it doesn't take away from your responsibility to the people in your immediate vicinity.

It's no accident that the people who Jesus praises in his story in Matthew 25 were already in the proximity of the "least of these." Note that when Jesus condemned those who didn't serve the least, he did it because they saw but did *not* act. It wasn't because they didn't know anyone who needed serving—it was because they looked the other way.

SANITIZATION

In Mark 1:40-45, a leper approached Jesus and asked to be made clean. This man was already breaking the law by even getting close to Jesus. Lepers were supposed to announce their presence by crying out "Unclean!" before passing through a public area. They had to sleep outside of the village. If they even touched somebody's house, it was supposed to be torn down because it was considered to be unclean. Nobody could come within ten feet of a leper. Can you imagine such an existence?

But this leper came up to Jesus and said, "Would you make me clean?" And Jesus doesn't turn away. The Scripture says he was moved with compassion and anger at what he perceived as unfair treatment. So Jesus reached out his hand and touched this man who had not been touched for who knows how many years. Not by his children, not by his spouse, not by his mother.

Let's be clear: Jesus didn't have to touch him. He was pretty good at miracle projection. He could have just said a word and the man would have been healed, but he reached out his hand and touched the man first, and then said, "Be clean."

Not only was Jesus not infected by this man's leprosy . . . it was the other way around. Jesus was so full of life and health that he infected the leper with his life. Jesus was more contagious with the life of the Kingdom than the leper was with his disease. And you know if the Spirit of God lives inside you, you're like that.

I know, I know. "But Harlow, this is Jesus we're talking about. He didn't have to worry about leprosy." True . . . he wasn't infected by leprosy. But then, Jesus was infected by our sin and willingly died of it, so we probably shouldn't use that as an excuse.

I'm not saying you shouldn't use hand sanitizer. I'm saying you shouldn't use a *heart* sanitizer. We fear sin sometimes, and rightly so in proper proportions, because it is a destructive thing, and we're called to be holy. But understand the message of Jesus. Sin is not nearly as contagious as the life of the Kingdom of God. Jesus just kept extending his hand—healing lepers, blessing children, washing feet—until, as Kyle Idleman says, they finally had to nail his hands down to get him to stop.

So put your book down and look at your hands for a moment. How often are they extended in service to someone who's far from God? Maybe you have a neighbor for whom you could mow the lawn or do an errand. Maybe there's somebody at work who feels discouraged, and these hands could write a note, and touch a heart. Maybe there's a lonely person in your world. Mother Teresa said that loneliness is the leprosy of our day. From busboys to CEOs, there are a lot lonely people. And maybe your hand is the one that could rest around their shoulders. You could notice them. You could listen to them.

I want to give you one caveat here as we talk about developing relationships with people far from God. Sometimes people think or wonder, "Is relational evangelism really a form of using people? Am I just pretending to be a friend so I can get a spiritual commitment out of somebody?"

You don't really have to worry about that. People can see through phoniness faster than you can say "Governor of Illinois." The obvious answer is "no." We can't help people unless we actually care about them.

When you get to know people, *really* know them, it's hard not to love them. When you start to love people, it's hard not to want the best for them. When you want the best for them, it's hard not to want to introduce them to Jesus.

In essence, you have no choice. If you love like Jesus, you are driven to do this. It is your mission. If my child were lost, I would do absolutely anything to get her home. And some day, when we're all gathered in heaven, I doubt that anyone is going to look you up and say, "You jerk. I can't believe you tricked me to get me here."

Filled with compassion, Jesus reached out his hand and touched the man. The Greek word for compassion here is a rich, power-packed word with much more color than our English word "compassion." It is an aching, painful word. It's the same word used to describe the Good Samaritan. The word in the Greek is Splachnizomai. The root is "Splach." Say that out loud. Even in the Greek—doesn't it sound gut-wrenching? It very literally means to hurt so much that you are moved to action.

Our hearts should break with the same things that break the heart of God.

CHAPTER 8

GOOD SAMARITAN (AND OTHER OXYMORONS)

"THE PEOPLE OF GOD ARE NOT MERELY TO MARK TIME, WAITING FOR GOD TO STEP IN AND SET RIGHT ALL THAT IS WRONG. RATHER, THEY ARE TO MODEL THE NEW HEAVEN AND NEW EARTH, AND BY SO DOING AWAKEN LONGINGS FOR WHAT GOD WILL SOMEDAY BRING TO PASS."

- PHILIP YANCEY

This story circulated awhile back in the Ozarks, where I went to college, about this old farmer. He was coming out of his field along the backroads in the hills, and just as he pulled out on the main road, a guy came speeding over the hilltop and hit his rig. The farmer ended up pinned under his wagon, his dog seriously injured not far away, and his poor mule across the road in the other ditch. The driver, who already had one D.U.I., high-tailed it out of there, just in time because the sheriff was the next car to come by. The farmer couldn't believe his luck in having the sheriff so close behind until he saw how the sheriff handled the situation.

Looking over the carnage, the sheriff saw the mule had a broken leg and was suffering badly, so he pulled out his revolver and shot it to end its misery. He walked across the road and saw the dog was just as bad off, so he shot him, too. Then he walked back over to the farmer and asked if he was in pain.

The farmer quickly replied, "Never felt better in my life!"

Unfortunately, when people are hurting, sometimes the last person they actually trust to help them is someone they ought to trust.

None of Jesus' parables (except perhaps the Prodigal Son) is better known, both in and outside the church, than the Good Samaritan. It's the story of the *wrong person helping when the right person couldn't be trusted.*

The Good Samaritan story was initially told as an answer to a question; an expert of the law asked it, not because he really wanted to know the answer, but because he was trying to test Jesus . . . to make him look bad in front of the people, and to put him on the spot. We will find out in a minute why you should not attempt to do this to the ruler of the universe, but for now—understand the attitude with which Jesus told this story. And why he picked a "good" Samaritan. Luke 10:

On one occasion an expert in the law stood up to test Jesus. "Teacher," he asked, "what must I do to inherit eternal life?"

"What is written in the Law?" he replied. "How do you read it?"

He answered, "'Love the Lord your God with all your heart and with all your soul and with all your strength and with all your mind'; and, 'Love your neighbor as yourself.'"

"You have answered correctly," Jesus replied. "Do this and you will live."

But he wanted to justify himself, so he asked Jesus, "And who is my neighbor?"

Jesus is as subtle as a sledgehammer in his telling of the story of the Good Samaritan.

Everyone loves the intrinsic drama of this story, but many people still miss the point. It's a dark story that we've heard too many times. One Sunday school teacher must have told it in better detail than mine ever did. She described the man's beating, how he was robbed and basically left for dead, in very vivid detail, wanting her students to grasp the full impact of this drama. Then it was pop quiz time. She asked the class, "If you saw a person lying on the roadside, all wounded and bleeding, what would you do?" A thoughtful little girl finally broke the hushed silence: "I think I'd throw up."

Well, that's more like it. So might we all, if we came face-to-face with the reality. A dark, lonely road. A victim of a vicious mugging. Maybe it's even a corpse . . . no, wait . . . it's moving . . . try to picture this as you drive along the road, at night.

The victim is in pretty bad shape, but never fear! In the story, a priest is the first guy on the scene. If our poor, battered soul has any consciousness at all—if he can see out of either bruise-swollen eye—he's thinking, like our farmer when the sheriff arrived: "Oh good, a man of God. Now I'm saved."

But wait. The priest decides not to get involved. On his theological list of "Things that make God happy"—well, somehow this situation didn't make the top ten. Or maybe he was just pragmatic; perhaps he had other places to go, other people to see. Maybe he had really, really important church business to attend to. Or, hey, he might have been just a tad judgmental: "Well, this guy did it to himself. Out here alone, carrying cash—what did he expect?" Finally, there's the fear factor: "What if he's a bad guy and I stop to help him? Could be a trick, to rip me off . . . " If Jesus were telling it today, there would be lawsuits to worry about.

So what does he do? *"A priest happened to be going down the same road, and when he saw the man, he passed by on the other side"* (Luke 10:31 NIV). That is, he had to go out of his way to keep from doing the right thing.

Well, there's always one slacker in any crowd, right? Not to worry, because, despite our initial disillusionment, our victim suddenly hears new footsteps up on the road.

More bad news. *"So too, a Levite, when he came to the place and saw him, passed by on the other side"* (Luke 10:32 NIV).

Another sheriff. Some days, it just doesn't pay to get out of bed.

Now the Levite, at least, has a theological basis for not getting involved. Priests of the Tribe of Levi officiated at the sacrifices that, in turn, allowed the people to participate in the presence of the Holy God. Under the Law of Moses, God's Chosen People had set up a strictly prescribed "purification" system. Levites had to be "pure" when they led the sacrifice, and one of the primary purification laws involves dead people.

Simply stated, this law said: don't touch 'em. Don't even go near 'em. So if our Levite does go over to help—if he merely rolls the victim over and then finds out the guy's dead—well, he's "contaminated" for the next seven days. Ergo, during that time he can't help the other people who really need him. So it's hasta la vista from our now rapidly departing Levite.

Okay, maybe I'm making excuses here, but doesn't everybody do this? Whenever we decide *not* help someone, we all have a perfectly "good" reason. There's a distinct possibility that both the priest and the Levite were simply setting priorities—that, in their minds, it was more important to try to please God (by following the rules) than to help people. It's illogical (and inconceivable, maybe even to God), but it wouldn't have been the first time, and won't be the last.

This was exactly the situation in which Jesus found himself when he healed a man on the Sabbath and the Pharisees got mad about it. Rule breaker.

A few moments now pass, during which our poor victim bleeds in quiet desperation.

Why did the religious guy cross the road? Because his priorities were jacked up.

And then, along comes a Samaritan.

Now the Jews and the Samaritans hated each other. "Good Samaritan?" This was the biggest oxymoron any Jew could envision. It was like "jumbo shrimp," "country music," or "Cubs win." It went deeper than most of us today could possibly understand. It simply wasn't possible to have a "good" Samaritan.

But this Samaritan stopped, squinted down at the moaning figure in the ditch, and, as Luke 10:33 describes it, he "had compassion."

Compassion, as we've seen already, is near to the heart of God. It's what should motivate us to do something, and our motivation is what matters most to God.

"He went to him and bandaged his wounds, pouring on oil and wine. Then he put the man on his own donkey, brought him to an inn and took care of him. The next day he took out two denarii and gave them to the innkeeper. 'Look after him,' he said, 'and when I return, I will reimburse you for any extra expense you may have'" (Luke 10: 34-35 NIV).

Jesus' amazing story was about the fact that the religious people, who should have been the first ones to reach out and help this man, were the ones who walked on the other side. I don't honestly believe that the story was about the guy who *did* help. It was an indictment of the two who *didn't*.

NOTHING WILL THWART OUR MISSION FASTER THAN THE PERCEPTION BY OUR JERUSALEM THAT WE DON'T CARE!

There are several things that stand out to me from this story. The first is that the Samaritan stopped. Too many of us simply don't. There have been lots of interesting psychological studies on this topic . . . sadly, without great conclusions.

Several years ago, two Princeton psychologists decided to conduct an experiment based on the story of the Good Samaritan. They met with a group of seminary students and asked them to prepare a short talk on a biblical theme, and then to walk over to a nearby building to present it.

Along they way, they set up a "situation." They planted a man who would be slumped down in an alley, head down, eyes closed, coughing and groaning. The "plant" would appear to be in obvious need of help. Naturally, our researchers wanted to see which seminary students would stop and help. To make it even more interesting, they built in three variables.

1. They first asked the motives of the people studying for ministry. Did they want to do ministry for personal spiritual fulfillment—or to help others? Unbeknownst to the seminarians, a preliminary questionnaire tested the motives of each student.
2. They had one group prepare a talk on the Role of Professional Clergy, and the other group on the story of the Good Samaritan.
3. They told one group that they needed to hurry, to rush to the presentation site because they were already late; they told the other group there was plenty of time to get to the auditorium.

Many of us might guess that those who entered the ministry to help others would have been more likely to help the man. I certainly would have guessed that those who had just heard the story of the Good Samaritan would surely have stopped to assist.

Nope. The psychologists found that neither of those variables mattered at all! According to the study's analysis: "On several occasions, a seminary student going to give his talk on the parable of the Good Samaritan literally stepped over the victim as he hurried on his way."

So what was the key here? Alas, the researchers discovered that the only variable that mattered was if the student had been told he or she was in a hurry. Only 10% of those in a hurry stopped, but 63% of those who had more time stopped to assist the "victim."[12]

Nothing has changed. It's not like the Samaritan had nothing better to do! According to the story Jesus told, the Samaritan was himself a man on the move, with places to go and people to see. Like any harried businessman, he was in a hurry.

I HONESTLY BELIEVE THAT THE GREATEST HINDRANCE TO THE MISSION OF JESUS IS THE BUSYNESS OF HIS AGENTS.

If you really dug into the hearts of most churches, you'd find people who care. But they have so much on their plates, much of which is actually church activity, that they literally don't feel like they can do anything but walk by on the other side. "Can't help you now, I've got to get to Bible Study."

Really?

THE MOST IMPORTANT THING MANY OF YOU READING THIS BOOK MIGHT BE ABLE TO DO TO GET BACK ON MISSION IS TO STOP GOING TO SO MANY BIBLE STUDIES.

Yep, I just said that.

The Samaritan took the time to stop, put the victim on his own donkey, and transported him to an inn. And it didn't end there: he took the time to hire someone to look after the victim, paid cash out-of-pocket for expenses, and even gave assurance that he would take the time to come back to cover the costs of any unforeseen medical tests and treatment.

It's important to note that the Samaritan then went on to do his business. He helped the man, even paid for the man's recovery, and then went about his own (presumably, urgent and important) business affairs.

Certainly, some of us will be called to give up our lives to work in the slums of Nairobi to help the less fortunate, but that's not the point of Jesus' story. The Samaritan didn't give up his life, or even his life savings. Given the monetary standards of the time, he gave up two weeks' pay—a couple of denarii—to help a person in need. That's not a trifle, but it's not the kids' college fund either. It was, simply stated, a case of giving what was needed, when it was needed, and for whom the need existed, to get the job done.

And it all happened, of course, because our Samaritan not only stopped... but he dropped. He got off his donkey (there are times I would rather preach from the King James, if you know what I mean).

To fulfill the spirit of what Jesus was teaching in the Good Samaritan tale, we, too, have to get off our . . . donkeys. We must recognize the needs of "the lesser among us," and then do the right thing in response to those needs.

Again, please remember that this story was in response to a supposed trick question—"And who is my neighbor?"

This isn't about our responsibility to the kids in another country—as much as I love those kids in Malawi and Bolivia. This is about the ones we have to go across the road to *avoid*!

The story's conclusion was a triple put-down to the expert in the law who posed the question. First, it made the neighbor an irrelevant stranger of no important standing, someone the Pharisees wouldn't have cared about. Second, it showed up their kind as totally insensitive to the situation (they were of the priests and Levites group who walked by on the other side). Third, it forced the expert in the law to have to conclude, by his own admission, that the hated Samaritan was the one with the example to be followed. Jesus' concluding statement "Go and do likewise" must have stung particularly hard. *"Go and model my life after a Samaritan?"* he must have been thinking. *"Not on your life."*

The question here is not about which person you ought to be, that's obvious. We need to be the guy who stopped and dropped.

Actually the question never changed. The original question was "Who is my neighbor?" *That's still it.* Who is lying in need around you right now? Who are you walking by and missing because you're not paying attention, or you just don't want to get involved?

I asked Lee Strobel about this topic recently, and he put it like this:

> *I think if Jesus physically lived in my house, he'd have a compassion radar that was scanning the neighborhood looking for opportunities to put his love into action. We can do that—we can have a compassion radar and maybe see the widow down the block that just wants someone to go to the grocery store with her once a week. It'd be such a blessing. Or the single mom that lives down the block and she's got two kids and she's working two jobs and she's barely staying afloat. If we said, "Hey, you know, what if my spouse and I watched your children for the next four Friday nights just so you can have some time to yourself?" Or maybe the compassion radar picks up a little kid down the block who has a basketball and hoop on his driveway, but nobody to shoot baskets with. What if we just shot some baskets with him?*
>
> *I think Jesus, if he physically lived in my house, he'd be looking for those opportunities, to not just say that he loves the world, but to put that love into action.*

It might be time to work on that compassion radar. It gets dull with lack of use. You grow accustomed to the shades over your eyes; you get used to ignoring that nagging prompting inside until you don't even feel it anymore. You're busy looking down at your phone and don't realize that you've actually crossed the road to avoid. I do it, too.

It's time to stop crossing the road.

CHAPTER 9

DON'T MAKE ME GET MY MILLSTONE

"If anyone causes one of these little ones—those who believe in me—to stumble, it would be better for them if a large millstone were hung around their neck and they were thrown into the sea" (Mark 9:42 NIV).

I need to tip my hand here about a couple of things. One, I recently got my first tattoo. I know that may not make you happy—Mom—but I wanted to make a statement. I'm not advocating marking yourself up. I just found no biblical reason not to (Leviticus is old covenant, right after the verse about how we shouldn't shave). It's a blend of Parkview's logo (which is a Celtic cross with wheat behind it, representing the fields ready for harvest), with the words "Heaven to Earth, Earth to Heaven" wrapped around it. That's my mantra.

This whole *serving* thing is a part of a bigger theological issue in which I firmly believe. Jesus did not teach that the Kingdom of Heaven is about getting people saved so we can get out of here when we die. Jesus taught the disciples that the Kingdom of Heaven is here, now, right in this place. Those of us that know Jesus are already experiencing the Kingdom—we have a bit of heaven on earth.

Once, on being asked by the Pharisees when the kingdom of God would come, Jesus replied, "The coming of the kingdom of God is not something that can be observed, nor will people say, 'Here it is,' or 'There it is,' because the kingdom of God is in your midst" (Luke 17:20 NIV).

And as believers, we are called to help bring heaven to earth. This is why we serve our neighbor. It's why we try to right the wrongs in this world.

But this earth will one day pass away, and those of us who have accepted the grace of Jesus on earth have been promised an eternity with him in heaven. So our mission is to bring *Heaven to Earth*, and take *Earth to Heaven*.

Life on Mission is about doing both. When you lighten someone's burden, you bring a bit of heaven to earth. When you ease someone's pain, feed someone who is hungry, provide medicine to someone who is sick, you are bringing heaven to earth. It's an outward representation of the kind of internal healing that happens through Jesus' abundant life. You are, in a sense, the gospel with clothes on.

When you bring heaven to earth, you earn the right to share the gospel and hopefully, eventually, bring earth to heaven.

Love your neighbor as yourself. So who is my neighbor? How can I bring heaven on earth to my neighbor? Well, I serve, and Jesus told me to serve the least of these. And who is the least of these?

How about we take that literally for a minute? If we're going to bring heaven to the least of these, it's about serving kids. I can't talk about serving without including this. I believe this comes from the heart of Jesus.

Back in the mid-1980s, a South African photojournalist by the name of Kevin Carter was on assignment in the famine-stricken country of Sudan. There he stumbled onto a scene that, in a single photograph, epitomized the horrific tragedy of world poverty.

> *"...Immediately after their plane touched down in the village of Ayod, Carter began snapping photos of famine victims. Seeking relief from the sight of masses of people starving to death, he wandered into the open bush. The sound of soft, high-pitched whimpering attracted Carter to an emaciated Sudanese toddler. The tiny girl had collapsed while struggling to a feeding center. As Carter crouched to photograph her, a vulture landed in view, a few paces behind the child.*
>
> *And the vulture waited, impassive.*

Carter later said that he watched through his camera's viewfinder for almost 20 minutes, hoping that the vulture would spread its wings. It didn't. Finally, Carter snapped the haunting photograph and chased the vulture away.

The photograph, sold to The New York Times, *appeared for the first time on March 26, 1993. Hundreds of people contacted the newspaper to ask whether the child had survived, leading the newspaper to run a special editor's note saying the girl had enough strength to walk away from the vulture—but that her ultimate fate was unknown..."*[13]

Maybe you remember seeing this photograph. No—strike that: if you *did*, you definitely *do*, because I can't imagine anyone who could ever forget it. Certainly, Mr. Carter couldn't. In 1994, three weeks after being awarded the Pulitzer Prize for the photo, the photographer committed suicide.

"I am haunted," his suicide note read, "by the vivid memories of killings and corpses and anger and pain . . . of starving or wounded children."

Some commentators noted that the photograph galvanized millions around the globe to the plight of hundreds of thousands of starving Sudanese who faced the same fate as the Sudanese toddler Carter was witnessing through his viewfinder. Without doubt, the subsequent flood of relief supplies certainly saved many lives, which otherwise very likely would have been lost. Additionally, Carter had been instructed not to touch any children, to avoid disease. He did his job.

But doesn't that sound like the religious people who avoided the wounded guy in the last chapter? Didn't Carter have a moral obligation to help the little girl to the feeding center in that moment?

I'm not judging Carter. That's not my job. He saw horrendous things many of us in America could comfortably avoid (including the Apartheid rule in South Africa). No wonder the poor guy felt tortured.

The philosopher Soren Kierkegaard, in discussing the moral obligations of Christians, described the tension between thought and action this way: "The Bible is very easy to understand, but we pretend to be unable to understand it, because we know very well that the minute we do, we are obligated to act accordingly."

Can you relate?

Let's stay on the subject of our moral obligation to serve children, specifically.

Jesus said, *"If anyone causes one of these little ones—those who believe in me—to stumble, it would be better for them if a large millstone were hung around their neck and they were thrown into the sea"* (Mark 9:42 NIV).

I don't know how much of Jesus' teaching you are familiar with, but this is pretty extreme. It sounds like an episode of *The Sopranos*. Or maybe *The Godfather*—"I'm going to make you an offer you can't refuse—take care of my kids, or else."

The millstone is a direct quote in Mark and Matthew. It's not one of those comments that anyone is going to quickly forget. Jesus was not mincing words. Wait—*it gets better*. Just a few days later, Mark 10:13 (NIV) tells us: *People were bringing little children to Jesus to have him touch them, but the disciples rebuked them. When Jesus saw this, he was indignant.*

Indignant. Definition: "Angry at injustice."

You can't help but think the next words were spoken with a raised pitch in his voice, Jesus' angry voice. You parents know the voice. If you've ever read this next verse out loud before, you probably did it in your nice, Grandma voice. But knowing that Jesus is "indignant" changes things. Say this next sentence out loud in your "indignant" voice, through clenched teeth: *"Let the little children come to me, and do not hinder them, for the kingdom of God belongs to such as these."* (Mark 10:14 NIV). Doesn't that change the verse for you?

It's as if Jesus is saying, "Don't you guys remember what we talked about? Don't make me get my millstone!"

He goes on to make his point as strongly as possible, and even threatens supernatural protection. *"See that you do not despise one of these little ones. For I tell you that their angels in heaven always see the face of my Father in heaven"* (Matthew 18:10 NIV).

This is one of the passages where people get the concept of a guardian angel. Jesus clearly is saying that the angels who look after the children are always focused on the face of God. Angels are somehow worshiping the Almighty God while they watch over all little children. Jesus knows that when you mess with kids, you are messing with a lot more than you bargain for. There is something very special about children, so ignoring children made Jesus angry. *"In the same way your Father in heaven is not willing that any of these little ones should perish"* (Matthew 18:14 NIV).

Don't you wonder how the angels are feeling now that 100 million children around the world live on the streets? Dr. Wess Stafford, former President of Compassion International, says, "The likelihood of a Haitian child surviving until his or her fifth birthday is so remote that some Haitian parents have adopted the practice of not naming their children until they are five years of age."

According to UNICEF, 21,000 children under age 5 die *every day*—not from horrible diseases or accidents, but from easily prevented disease, malnutrition, and lack of provision. They die from being poor.[14]

I know, it's not your fault they are poor, but aren't we supposed to do more than take a picture?

Psalm 82:3-4 (NLT) says, *"Give justice to the poor and the orphan; uphold the rights of the oppressed and the destitute. Rescue the poor and helpless; deliver them from the grasp of evil people."* That's pretty much a command.

I would have to admit that for most of my life, I've been . . . let's just say . . . indifferent. I'm sure some of it was immaturity, but some of it was just sinfulness. It was selfishness. Somewhere in my sinful heart I thought, "I've got mine. I've got food and clothing and shelter. My kids are okay. Hope things work out for you."

But there are more red letters in my Bible that seem pretty pointed on this subject. In another passage Jesus tells us exactly what he expects of us: *"Then he will say to those on his left, 'Depart from me, you who are cursed, into the eternal fire prepared for the devil and his angels. For I was hungry and you gave me nothing to eat, I was thirsty and you gave me nothing to drink, I was a stranger and you did not invite me in, I needed clothes and you did not clothe me, I was sick and in prison and you did not look after me.' They also will answer, 'Lord, when did we see you hungry or thirsty or a stranger or needing clothes or sick or in prison, and did not help you?' He will reply, 'Truly I tell you, whatever you did not do for one of the least of these, you did not do for me'"* (Matthew 25:41-45 NIV).

It really only started sinking in for me when I got out of my own comfort zone. For many years I told God I would do mission trips "later." Finally, when I could put him off no longer, I went to see life on the other side. Don't get me wrong—you do not have to go far to find kids in need. There are probably some close to you. There are by me. But I knew I needed to get our church more interested in the world, so I started to venture out there. I've now seen poverty up close in Chicago, Cuba, Costa Rica, Ecuador, Mexico, Dominican Republic, Rwanda, Bolivia, and most recently, in Kenya. It changes you.

There is nothing like the slums of Nairobi. There is nothing like the smell. There is no way to describe to you how bad the living conditions are. My then-21-year-old daughter, Lauren, wrote about it:

> At the school our church supports, our van pulled up to a thick, stone wall that stood about 15 feet high. This landmark that would not meet safety codes in the states separated the school from the surrounding slums, and it made me uneasy. This was not the sight of the haven I expected, nor was it safe or clean or even a bit classy. I had wanted the school to at least look reliable, because then I could assume the African kids were taken care of. And if they were taken care of, than surely they would not judge me for being groomed, or having nice clothes, or for the fact that I had enough money to fly 26 hours to see them.
>
> As we walked through the slums, we were encouraged to talk with people. Our leader promised they would be welcoming, but I did not believe her. We turned a corner and I met the gaze of a two-year old girl. I bent down and gently poked her belly. She did not smile. She looked at me and made it clear she was busy chewing on a piece of trash, and was in no mood to play. There was crust dried around her mouth and her brown velvet dress was decorated similarly with grime. Her twin sister stood behind her, skeptically examining my skin. I made some kids laugh and some cry, depending on if they liked my skin or if it scared them. In another alleyway, there was a little boy sitting on an island of dirt. Around the small mound were pieces of wrappers and plastic bags. We were warned especially not to step on the plastic bags, also known as "flying toilets." It would not be sanitary, to say the least, to smash one of these plastic sewage systems. But the little boy on the mound did not seem to mind.

Our lives were changed by this trip. The crazy thing about me is that I've always loved kids. I just didn't know these kids yet. I love the kids I know. If a kid in my neighborhood falls and hurts himself, I'm going to run over and help him, because that's the kind of guy I am. I'm not going to callously say, "Well, you shouldn't have been trying to jump over that SUV in your rollerblades."

But when 6,000 kids in the world become orphans *every day* because of AIDS, I'm not there. I don't see it. I don't *know* them. Today there are an estimated 143 million orphans in the world. Let's do some math. Christianity is ranked as the largest religion in the world today with approximately 2.3 billion adherents. If roughly 6% of the Christians in the world would adopt, there would be no more orphans.

I'm not here to tell you what to do. (Okay, maybe I am.) Adoption is a long, expensive, emotionally exhausting process—if you've done it or are in the process now, God bless you a million times over. But I think you would have to be very hard-pressed to not be able to come up with a dollar a day to sponsor a child through an agency.

Bottom line, find a way to take care of kids. I know our focus is on our Jerusalem and it feels like we've strayed a little on this topic, but you don't have to leave your Jerusalem to be involved. You don't have to leave your Jerusalem to sponsor a kid. And the kids who need help are not all in other countries!

Is there a child around you that you could mentor? Could you serve in your church's children's ministry?

Even if you decide that you don't like your neighbors and don't want to spend eternity with them, you can still do something to be on mission with the "least of these."

"Truly I tell you, whatever you did not do for one of the least of these, you did not do for me" (Matthew 25:45 NIV).

"In the same way your Father in heaven is not willing that any of these little ones should perish" (Matthew 18:14 NIV).

James 1:27 (NIV) tells us that, *Religion that God our Father accepts as pure and faultless is this: to look after orphans and widows in their distress and to keep oneself from being polluted by the world.*

Statistics tell us that the vast majority of people become believers as children. If we're going to be on mission, we'd better not neglect serving the *really* least.

SHARE

CHAPTER 10

HOLY SET-UPS

How then shall they call on him in whom they have not believed? and how shall they believe in him whom they have not heard? and how shall they hear without a preacher? (Romans 10:14 ASV)

It *is* about you (with apologies to Rick Warren).

You are a major part of God's plan for saving the world. No pressure or anything, but it's true, and it's brilliant at the same time. The reason you don't have to feel all the pressure is because you're not alone (there are a lot of God's agents working with you), and the Holy Spirit is working in and through you, and in the lives of the people you talk to about Christ. So it's not all up to you.

Actually, Rick and I agree—but let me put it together:
YOUR PURPOSE IS NOT ABOUT YOU—IT'S ABOUT
GOD'S KINGDOM—WHICH IS ABOUT YOU—USING
GOD'S POWER AND HIS GIFTS TO LIVE OUT YOUR
MISSION. Capisce?

As a matter of fact, once God's plan for your mission gets rolling, you will discover that God is pretty much taking you for a ride, and it's the biggest adventure of your life. In the process, you will be aware of your responsibility to represent the gospel, but you will also be aware of something miraculous that takes over once you begin.

Think about it. God entrusted his new church based on Jesus Christ in the hands of about 120 followers, and they were under the leadership of twelve guys who I don't think anyone would believe were the sharpest knives in the drawer. I mean no disrespect, but re-read the Gospels sometime. None of this would have happened if it was all up to them—it had to be the Holy Spirit. Then again, none of this would have happened if they just sat at home and played Xbox® either. God uses men and women who step up to the plate.

Before we get further into this next section, let's recap our mission thus far.

CONNECT: We hang out with "tax collectors and sinners." Without discriminating or judging, we reach out to the people around us. Invite people into our homes. That part is a little scary for some, but I don't know anyone who has a problem with eating pizza for God. *Check.*

SERVE: We put our love and faith into action by getting a little messy. We go out of our way to make life easier for those around us. We serve, not just because it's a great way for people to see God's love, but also because we're driven by compassion for the hurting and because Jesus told us to in no uncertain terms. This is hard and often inconvenient, but you probably won't create any enemies by serving. *Check.*

Part three?

If we have connected in the backyard, and served by inviting them into the house, at some point they are going to start asking us some important questions.

That means it's time to invite them to sit at the kitchen table and have a chat.

HOLY TIP-OFFS
In this chapter, we're going to take a look at one of the original 120, and see what we can learn from his story—what happens when our willingness meets God's omnipotence. His name is Phillip, one of the disciples who had been with Jesus from the beginning.

Those who had been scattered preached the word wherever they went. Philip went down to a city in Samaria and proclaimed the Messiah there. When the crowds heard Philip and saw the signs he performed, they all paid close attention to what he said. For with shrieks, impure spirits came out of many, and many who were paralyzed or lame were healed (Acts 8:4-7 NIV).

Remember when Jesus told these early disciples that they would be his witnesses *"in Jerusalem, and in all Judea and Samaria, and to the ends of the earth"* (Acts 1:8 NIV)? Well, I guess Philip drew the Samaria straw. We've already established the bad blood for Samaria. I'm doubting anyone said, "Ooh, Samaria, pick me." But with the help of the Spirit, it didn't take him long to create a stir. The people were seeing something genuine. Philip's message about the Messiah was appealing (the Samaritans were looking for the Messiah just like the Jews. Remember the Samaritan woman's words to her whole town: "Could this be the Messiah?"). But there were also supernatural miracles happening in the natural world.

There was what Philip said, and there was what Philip did—they complemented each other. A powerful witness will have both.

The key to sharing the love of Jesus is living a life that people want to know more about. We're not talking about a perfect life, just a real one that can't quite be explained without God.

You may not have the gift of physical healing or casting out demons. But you do have the Holy Spirit, and he should be evident in your life. It could be courage in the midst of fear, strength in the midst of weakness, joy in the midst of sorrow, or perhaps more than anything, hope, because not too many people have much hope anymore. These qualities are unusual and attractive, and when they catch someone's eye, that person might just be willing to listen to what you have to say.

Now an angel of the Lord said to Philip, "Go south to the road— the desert road—that goes down from Jerusalem to Gaza" (Acts 8:26 NIV).

Stop right there! Are you feeling a little jealous? I don't know about you, but I read that and think—good grief, I would love directions that clear! I wonder if the voice sounded like Siri. "In 37 cubits, turn left."

Denise and I had an experience like this in the beginning of our ministry. We were living in St. Louis with our two-year-old daughter Rachel, not too far from Denise's parents, when we went to Chicago to interview with Tinley Park Church of Christ (now Parkview Christian Church). When we returned to our hotel room that night, we both broke down and wept. We knew. We absolutely *knew*. We didn't want to move, we loved where we were. Really, nobody moves to Chicago . . . in JANUARY! . . . unless God's calling.

For us, there wasn't another option. God told us to go. We didn't hear an audible voice, but we may as well have for the crystal clarity we had in that moment. It's the most profound call we've had, and 24 years later we can attest that it was the right call.

Here is what's so cool about listening to the voice of God. The Lord did more than direct Phillip to a place, he actually set up an encounter. I could tell countless stories of God-directed encounters in the lives of people I know. If this isn't something you've experienced before, well... brace yourself. It's coming. If the Holy Spirit is in you, it is coming. It may have already happened, you just didn't catch it. The more you learn to pay attention to the Holy Spirit, the more you will pick up on these subtle—and sometimes not-so-subtle—promptings. But brace yourself, because when the moment comes, the instructions may be bizarre and uncomfortable, and you may be tempted to run away rather than obey.

Philip obeyed, and look how it went down:

> So he started out, and on his way he met an Ethiopian eunuch, an important official in charge of all the treasury of the Kandake (which means "queen of the Ethiopians"). This man had gone to Jerusalem to worship, and on his way home was sitting in his chariot reading the Book of Isaiah the prophet. The Spirit told Philip, "Go to that chariot and stay near it."

Then Philip ran up to the chariot and heard the man reading Isaiah the prophet. "Do you understand what you are reading?" Philip asked.

"How can I," he said, "unless someone explains it to me?" So he invited Philip to come up and sit with him (Acts 8:27-31 NIV).

Is this a set-up or what? See what God can do when you're tuned in to the Holy Spirit? This is an influential man. He was in charge of all the treasury of Candace, queen of the Ethiopians. God wanted a Christian in the ruling class of Ethiopia. This is the gospel's doorway into Africa! How big is that? I'm actually working on this chapter from Rwanda right now. Christianity has changed this country and greatly affected the entire continent. Think about it, in some ways it all started with one guy named Phillip—open to the Spirit.

Notice how the Lord put Phillip right next to the chariot. He didn't tell him what to do, he just put him within earshot of the Ethiopian reading Isaiah because he knew Philip could take it from there. It seems amazing, yet I believe the Lord does this to us all the time. When we know we're on a mission we'll be ready for stuff like this. If we're completely absorbed in life's minutia—getting to the next meeting on time, getting the kids' uniforms washed before tomorrow—who knows what we might be missing? That stuff has to happen; I live in the real world, too. But when we seek the Kingdom first instead of what's at the end of our noses, when we let God interrupt us…incredible things happen. In light of eternity, some of our deadlines lose their place at the top of our priority list.

So—are you listening? Are you willing to be interrupted? Are you willing to run alongside an important government official (or boss, or neighbor) because God told you to perk up your ears? Most of the Christians I know say that they haven't heard

God speak audibly the way Philip did, but a person trying to live life under God's direction will sometimes sense God prompting towards an action or an inquiry. I believe the Spirit directs us a lot more than we pay attention to.

For me recently, it was walking through the health club. I saw this huge, biker dude. He was the kind of guy who just looked like he could crush you with his pinky. I said "Hey man, how ya doing?"—which was really just my way of saying, "Dear sir, if I am in your way, please don't kill me—I'll move."

He shocked me by saying, "Not so good, I probably ought to come and see you." WELL! Either this guy thinks I'm a drug dealer, or he knows who I am. So I did something crazy, I gave him my cell number. You may not think that sounds crazy—but if I could show you the past several years' text conversations, you would be amazed. More inappropriate language than Southpark.

He's a believer now, and God is working in his life and through his life. But it all started when God sent me to work out at the same time and in the same vicinity as Mike, and prompted me to say these *deeply* insightful words . . . "Hey man, how ya doin'?"

Just like God sent Phillip. "Hey man, whatcha readin'?"

This is the passage of Scripture the eunuch was reading:

> *"He was led like a sheep to the slaughter,*
> *and as a lamb before its shearer is silent,*
> *so he did not open his mouth.*
> *In his humiliation he was deprived of justice.*
> *Who can speak of his descendants?*
> *For his life was taken from the earth."*

The eunuch asked Philip, "Tell me, please, who is the prophet talking about, himself or someone else?" Then Philip began with

*that very passage of Scripture and told him the good news
about Jesus* (Acts 8:32-35 NIV).

Talk about tossing up a soft ball! If the Holy Spirit tells you to talk
to someone, and his first question is "Tell me about Jesus," well,
how hard can it be?

The Ethiopian man gave Philip the perfect entry to talk about
the gospel. And I think this is key: Philip knew the life-changing
truth about Jesus, but he listened to the Ethiopian's questions
to determine how to communicate it. The man asked Philip
a question about the passage he was reading from Isaiah, and
"Philip began with this same passage of Scripture and then used
many others to tell him the good news about Jesus."

I'm not against programs that teach you how to share the gospel
in "ten timely truths" or the "4 spiritual laws" or whatever. Some
programs are helpful to teach us how to share our faith, but we
can't be tied to them.

Philip didn't begin with a prepared speech or an evangelistic
formula. He began with the Ethiopian man's questions and
concerns. He didn't say, "I see you are reading Isaiah—can I ask
you a question? If you died tonight, do you know if you would go
to heaven?"

I once heard someone say, "The best evangelistic tools you have
are stuck on the side of your head: your ears." If you are listening,
people will often hint—or even outright tell you—what their big
concerns are. Once you know them, you can ask more questions
that allow you to relate the gospel to their lives. Again, we learn
from the Master. Jesus was always asking questions.

Philip also didn't beat around the bush. It's important to be
sensitive to those with whom we're attempting to share the gospel,
but we don't do them any favors if we dance around the truth,

either. We can become so concerned about offending people that we don't speak with clarity.

Philip took him to Jesus. That can be uncomfortable. The name of Jesus is powerful. It saves, it soothes, but it sometimes offends. It's not Jesus' fault, it's the bad impression left by many of his followers. But . . . *"Salvation is found in no one else, for there is no other name under heaven given to mankind by which we must be saved"* (Acts 4:12 NIV).

It's always best to take the simplest approach. If the answer is Jesus, tell them about Jesus.

Acts 8 doesn't record all that Philip said to the Ethiopian, but we know Philip said it clearly because the man listening understood it. He was enthusiastic and responsive, and the man himself was even able to articulate the next step. Verse 36 informs us that the Ethiopian said, "Look! There's some water. Why can't I be baptized?" Apparently, Philip had explained the message of Christ so convincingly that this man knew what the next step should be, and he was ready to take that step.

If your audience is receptive, it's usually best to just tell them what they need to know. I'm not talking about being abusive or abrasive. It just never does any good to beat around the bush. If Jesus said he is the way, the truth, and the life, then he IS the way, the truth and the life. There is no other way to God. If there were, God would have never let Jesus die on the cross.

It was the Ethiopian who saw the water and said, "Let's do this." Don't you love that?

If you want to live on mission, be ready for adventure. You can't imagine all that God wants to do. Our evangelism plans are way too small. If you achieve what you projected, you probably didn't get all that the Lord had for you—the One who wants to do *immeasurably more than all we ask or imagine* (Ephesians 3:20 NIV).

Philip didn't go to Samaria because he knew there was a good chance that a high-ranking official of the Ethiopian government was going to be traveling on the road from Jerusalem to Gaza and he was hoping to get an opportunity to talk to him. He could have never guessed that! He went to Samaria because God told him to.

We need to listen carefully and keep an eye out for what the Holy Spirit might be doing. What has he already set up for you? Live this way, and I guarantee your life will be one adventure after another.

"Don't you have a saying, 'It's still four months until harvest'?" Jesus asked the disciples as the Samaritan woman he met at the well of Jacob was bringing the whole town up to the hillside to meet him. *"I tell you, open your eyes and look at the fields! They are ripe for harvest"* (John 4:35 NIV).

There is no shortage of crop, only a shortage of workers. Show up in your field ready to share, and you will have more opportunities than you will know what to do with.

CHAPTER 11

SAY UNCLE!

"Let me tell you what he has done for me" (Psalm 66:16 NIV).

Eugene Peterson is a pastor, scholar, author and poet who has written over thirty books—though, to be fair, one of them was the Bible, so it would only be right to up his book total to 96.

Yes, he wrote the whole Bible. Not the first time, obviously (so gullible!), but he translated it into what is now known as *The Message*, a modern paraphrase of the whole Bible. No small feat. When asked to explain why he took on the task, he said,

> *When Paul of Tarsus wrote a letter, the people who received it understood it instantly. When the prophet Isaiah preached a sermon, I can't imagine that people went to the library to figure it out. That was the basic premise under which I worked. I began with the New Testament in the Greek—a rough and jagged language, not so grammatically clean. I just typed out a page the way I thought it would have sounded to the Galatians.*[15]

Now why is this important? It's important because I want you to know who this guy is before I let you in on a story about his first convert—Garrison Johns, the second grade bully.

> *I had been prepared for life in my neighborhood and school by memorizing "Bless those who persecute you" and "Turn the other cheek." I don't know how Garrison Johns knew that about me, but he had figured it out. After school he would catch me and beat me up. I arrived home most afternoons bruised and humiliated. My mother told me this had always been the way of Christians in the world, and that I had better get used to it. I was also supposed to pray for him.*
>
> *One day when I was with seven or eight friends, he caught up with us and started pushing me. That's when*

it happened. Something snapped. For a moment, the Bible verses disappeared from my consciousness, and I grabbed Garrison Johns. To my surprise and his, I was stronger than he was. I threw him to the ground, sat on his chest, and pinned his arms with my knees. He was helpless and at my mercy. I hit him in the face with my fists. It felt good, so I hit him again. Blood spurted from his nose, a lovely crimson in the snow. I said, "Say uncle!" He wouldn't say it. I hit him again, more blood. Then my Christian training reasserted itself: "Say, I believe in Jesus Christ as my Lord and Savior!" He wouldn't say it. I hit him again, more blood. I tried again, "Say, I believe in Jesus Christ as my Lord and Savior!"—and he said it. Garrison Johns was my first convert.[16]

Now, your conversion may not have been a scene from *A Christmas Story*. Mine wasn't quite that epic. But think back for a moment about the person who did work up the courage to share Jesus with you.

Hopefully they weren't sitting on top of you hitting you in the face, but they did tell you about Jesus. It may have been your mom, who also occasionally lost her temper and said things she didn't mean. It may have been that friend, the frat brother from way back who got in all kinds of trouble before finding his own way to Christ. The neighbor you heard cursing at his yippy dog just this morning (the dog deserved it).

The point is, none of these people were models of perfection. They probably didn't come to you with a flawless dissertation on the divinity of Jesus. They may even have used language as rough and jagged as the original disciples, who were sailors, for crying out loud. But they shared.

And so should you.

Ed Stetzer wrote this recently in an article titled "Stop Talking Yourself Out of Evangelism":

Saying "preach the gospel; when necessary, use words" is a lot like saying "feed the hungry; when necessary, use food." Both are silly when people need bread—and the bread of life. So proclaim it. Out loud. To people without Christ.

The problem is that people probably aren't going to guess their way to the Good News. For all they know, you're only doing nice things because you want good Karma. You could seem peaceful because you spend a lot of time meditating in the moonlight—or smoking pot! We know the difference between "feeling calm" and having the Prince of Peace who stands by you when the storm is raging . . . but others don't.

How will they know unless we tell them?

The church started in Acts 2, when the Holy Spirit of God showed up and caused a ruckus, and Peter got up to explain what was going on. Peter was the recipient of grace. Jesus reinstated him after he failed miserably and he became the leader of the church. So Peter had a story. He got up and told it and the church got started.

"You are God's instruments to do His work and to speak out for Him and to tell others of the difference that He has made for you." That is 1 Peter 2:9—(paraphrased in the words of the guy who bloodied Garrison John's nose when he was seven.)

YOU HAVE A STORY

Alan Hirsch is a leader in the Missional Church movement. He was 18 when somebody first had the guts to share the gospel with him. Here's how he remembers it:

> *When I went to the military, I was called up. In order to kind of deal with the military, I did a lot of drugs. I think Jesus had to settle me down first before I could get into the kingdom. In our little drug circle there was this guy called Murry. Murry was the leader of our group. We'd sit around talking about the cosmos and kinds of things that druggies do.*

Murry became a Christian. He had an encounter with Jesus and the Holy Spirit one week, and he came back a completely transformed kind of guy. I remember him introducing me to this very person that had been wooing me all my life. I think that's the first time I ever heard the gospel being shared in my life. I knew it was right and it actually reset the agenda of my entire life at that point; eventually I came to a place of conversion.

The gospel showed through the life of a really good, quality person. He was a good guy before. He just became even better. He didn't judge us for what we were doing. He remained part of our circle. He remained our friend. I think that's one of the most powerful things.[17]

Eugene Peterson has a story. Garrison Johns has a story. Alan Hirsch has a story.

You have a story.

What you need to *share* is your story. The great thing about sharing your story is that no one can argue with your story. You don't need a degree in theology—you are already an expert! No one knows it better than you. And you don't have to embellish or hide the mistakes and fears, because you are not the hero of the story. See where I'm going with this?

We can all relate to the bleak emptiness of losing someone we love, whether by death or abandonment. We relate to seasons of financial crisis and feelings of desperation and worry. We've all experienced feeling insignificant or obsolete. We have all made stupid mistakes we've lived to regret.

These things make us human—our shared experiences. You don't have to hide the parts where you felt afraid or messed up. Those are the best parts, the parts that I connect with!

Where your story takes a turn for the better, though, is that your hope was not swallowed up by despair. You didn't lose sight of your true identity when you lost your job. You found a meaning to your existence that transcended that relationship or that crisis. You learned that you were seen, known, and loved in spite of it all.

People want to hear about it, probably more than you realize.

WHO MADE YOUR MOUTH?

If you're feeling intimidated by this whole speaking out thing—don't be discouraged. I've got a couple of passages of scripture for you to lean on. Put these somewhere you'll see them, or memorize them, if you can.

Here's the first, from the Old Testament prophet Isaiah:

> *As the rain and the snow*
> *come down from heaven,*
> *and do not return to it*
> *without watering the earth*
> *and making it bud and flourish,*
> *so that it yields seed for the sower and bread for the eater,*
> *so is my word that goes out from my mouth:*
> *It will not return to me empty,*
> *but will accomplish what I desire*
> *and achieve the purpose for which I sent it*
> (Isaiah 55:10-11 NIV).

You aren't advancing your own Kingdom. You aren't sharing the Gospel of Tim (or the Gospel of whoever). This is God's Kingdom, God's gospel, and God's message. You are bearing witness to your own experience, but the protagonist of the story isn't you, it's Jesus!

God's word isn't going to come up empty; it will get results. But this is key: those results are up to God, not us. We may think that this perfect opportunity to share the good news with another person should immediately result in his desire to repent and be saved . . . but the soil of his heart may not be ready. We'll talk about this more later in the book, but for now, just remember that you don't control the outcome of your obedience. You can only choose to be obedient in your role. Share your story, share God's truth, and God will accomplish through it exactly what he desires.

Here's the second, and this is one of my favorites. It's passages like this that convince my son-in-law, Ash, that God is British, because of his great use of sarcasm. God has just attracted Moses' attention through the famous burning bush, and Moses is a little (okay, a lot) resistant to God's command to go and speak to Pharaoh. Here's a bit of the dialogue:

> Moses said to the Lord, "Pardon your servant, Lord. I have never been eloquent, neither in the past nor since you have spoken to your servant. I am slow of speech and tongue."
>
> The Lord said to him, "Who gave human beings their mouths? Who makes them deaf or mute? Who gives them sight or makes them blind? Is it not I, the Lord? Now go; I will help you speak and will teach you what to say" (Exodus 4:10-12 NIV).

Translation: "I'm God, you imbecile! I can help you!"

It's embarrassing and comforting at the same time, isn't it? We don't want God to have to scold us like a kid in time-out, but his words are such an immense relief. Thank God. You're with me. Okay, you're going to help me speak and teach me what to say…I can get behind that. I can do this.

Jesus also said something similar when he sent out the disciples in Luke 21:14-15 (NIV). He tells them not to worry when they are brought into the courts. "But make up your mind not to worry beforehand how you will defend yourselves. For I will give you words and wisdom that none of your adversaries will be able to resist or contradict."

You can do this! The early church explosion started with a single sermon, preached by a brash, short-tempered fishmonger with no formal education. God will give you the words, and his word doesn't return empty.

Who made your mouth, anyway? You got this.

And check this out . . . when Jesus left the earth to go back to heaven, he said, *"You will be my witnesses in Jerusalem, and in all Judea and Samaria, and to the ends of the earth"* (Acts 1:8 NIV). Again, this was not for a select group of people; he said it to everyone in the small group of believers who were meeting together in those days following the resurrection. The group was numbered at around 120 people (Acts 1:15) and would have, undoubtedly, included people just like us. Those were the people he called to be his witnesses.

He called them witnesses. *You will be my witnesses. All 120 of you.* You are all qualified because of what you've seen and experienced. You are not my defense attorneys; you are not my prosecutors; you are not my salespersons. If I needed any of these I'd go hire them, but I only need a witness and you qualify.

A witness is somebody who simply tells what they have seen. "I saw this, I heard that, and then this happened to me." A witness is someone who has personal knowledge of what they speak.

The woman at the well didn't have answers, she had a testimony. Jesus once healed a man who had been blind from birth. Because the religious leaders heard about it and wanted to discredit Jesus, they began pelting the poor man with questions about his parents, about Jesus, and about himself, to the point of calling Jesus a sinner and the man, one of his followers.

Imagine you've been blind your entire life, and not even minutes after you can see for the first time you are being put through the theological ringer by a bunch of seminary professors about the man who just miraculously gave you sight. I bet your response would be similar to his: *"Whether he is a sinner or not, I don't know. One thing I do know. I was blind but now I see!"* (John 9:25 NIV).

There it is—the power of a simple witness. "I can't answer the deep questions of the universe. I can't tell you why there is sin and evil in the world. I don't know who Cain married. I DON'T KNOW! But I can tell you this—five minutes ago I was blind. I've been blind for over 30 years. I was just minding my own business when this stranger came up to me, put mud on my eyes and told me to go wash my face, and when I did . . . I could see! Put that in your pipe and smoke it" (my paraphrase).

Truth be told, when something truly miraculous happens to you, you can't *not* talk about it. If you'd been healed of blindness, would you *maybe* post that on Facebook? "You will be my witnesses" could be the easiest thing you've ever done. Just tell what you know.

You are like that man. You are the expert on your own life. No seminary training required. Nobody can be a better witness about what has happened to you than you.

You're not the prophet. You're not the preacher. You don't have to win a debate. You don't have to take back America. You don't have to have the last word on the definition of marriage. You don't need to explain creation versus evolution, and you don't have to apologize for bad-haired televangelists. *You just tell what you know.*

So if you haven't been invited up to the stand, how do you do it? How do you bring it up?

Three powerful words: "I can relate."

Paul opens up his letter to the church in Corinth with these words: *Praise be to the God and Father of our Lord Jesus Christ, the Father of compassion*

*and the God of all comfort, who comforts us in all our troubles,
so that we can comfort those in any trouble with the comfort we
ourselves receive from God* (2 Corinthians 1:3-4 NIV).

If you've ever wondered why your particular story includes
heartache or struggle or burnout or crisis, it might just be that
God wants you to be able to comfort someone else dealing with a
similar situation.

One of my favorite Old Testament stories is the life of Joseph.
Basically, everything that happens in Joseph's life (up until the
climax of the story) is brutally unfair—he's beaten up and sold into
slavery by his brothers, then wrongfully accused of assault and
sent to prison for several years. If you're familiar with the story,
you know that eventually, because of his obedience and integrity
and because God gives him wisdom to interpret a dream, Joseph
ends up as Pharaoh's second-in-command.

When those same brothers are forced to seek food in Egypt
because of a famine and encounter the brother they sold into
slavery, Joseph speaks these words to them, some of my favorite
in the entire Bible: *"You intended to harm me, but God intended it
for good to accomplish what is now being done, the saving of many
lives"* (Genesis 50:20 NIV).

Someone may have intended to harm you along the way. In some
cases, you may have been harmed as collateral damage. There are
probably situations from your past that you wish you could alter
and would remove from your memory, if you could.

Please . . . let God use it. He can, and he will.

Romans 8:28 tells us that he works ALL THINGS for the good of
those who love him and are called according to his purpose. God's
purpose is to further his kingdom, and he wants to do that *through
you*. Through your story. The good, the bad, and the ugly.

Lean on your shared human experience. Don't forget—you're not the attorney, and you're not the judge. You're just the witness.

One thing I know . . . I was blind, and now I see.

CHAPTER 12

DESTINATION: CALIFORNIA

"YOU MISS 100% OF THE SHOTS
YOU DON'T TAKE."

- WAYNE GRETZKY

Do you ever read stories from some hyper evangelist-type pastor or author who tells you about leading someone to Christ in an airplane ride conversation? You know, like "I struck up a conversation and then I got out a napkin and explained the *cross-bridge* to God and they got saved."

That's not me. I have to be honest. When I get on a plane, I don't pray for God to send me a seatmate whom I can guide to Jesus. I pray for an empty seat. I'm sorry, I know about eternity and my mission and all of that. I'm just telling you where I live. If there is someone next to me, I'm not hoping they say "Tell me about Jesus," I'm hoping they say "No hablo Inglés." Then I'm off the hook.

Sometimes God overrides me and I really do try to obey his prompting when it happens. But it never seems as easy as those "evangelist types" make it seem. If everyone were as receptive as Biker Mike or the Ethiopian Treasurer, we'd all be doing this a lot more. Many times, we talk to people who've been overexposed to the hypocritical nature of human Christians, or they've been hurt by the church, and they just don't want to hear about "the bridge."

I'm not saying that we shouldn't use God-ordained short encounters when they show up. That was literally Phillip's experience. What I'm saying is that often, as the landing gear goes back down, this person I have had no relationship with will say something like, "Well, I guess we're all just taking different paths to the same goal. All roads lead to the same place, right?"

Which is obviously so wrong that you want to say—"Do you see that plane over there? It's not going to the same place as this plane. That's why we need a ticket to the RIGHT PLACE, and we need to get on the RIGHT PLANE!"

But arguing is never going to work.

This is why I am a bigger proponent of relationship. Because most people have issues that take time to work through. Most answers need time to simmer.

The truth is, as shocking as this may seem, I've found that the Jesus approach is best. What did he do? Instead of always giving answers, he often asked more questions. Questions are good! Encourage as many questions as you can. Real questions. Sometimes you have to get through the stock questions to get to the real question.

Everyone has unspoken questions behind the one they're asking. When they ask, "Why would a good God allow evil in the world?" it's because they know something of the evil in the world.

Questions are probably our most valuable resource when we are in a conversation about spiritual matters. Our tendency is to want to get the conversation over with and see how it goes because we're uncomfortable.

But this comes off more as an argument than a discussion. I wouldn't consider myself a good counselor if all I did was tell people things and never listen to them. As a matter of fact, that's why I'm not a good counselor and we have other people on staff to do it! If Christians mess anything up in sharing our faith, it's because we are not being sensitive to the other person.

Consider the basic communication skills needed in marriage. Listen to Drs. Les and Leslie Parrott (who actually are good counselors):

> In order to understand better and communicate more effectively with our partner, we have to slow down and think. Good communication takes time. When the best-selling business book "The One Minute Manager" was popular, there were a hundred spin-offs, including "The One Minute Marriage." Give me a break. Maybe managers can accomplish their goals through quick contacts, but a husband and wife? Not likely.

When we slow down the conversation with our partner, we are less likely to give hasty orders, snappy solutions, and thoughtless comments. When we slow down, we are more likely to listen to the emotions that underlie our partner's words and pay more attention to the nonverbal messages. Taking care in these ways helps us avoid foolish conversations and brings about true understanding.[18]

I love the word "witness" because it implies that we are only called to tell what we know. The unfortunate part of many Christians' understanding of that word is that they are only responsible for telling—and not for communicating.

I love this quote from George Bernard Shaw: "The single biggest problem in communication is the illusion that it has taken place."[19] I can't tell you how many times I've "told" someone something, but it never got "communicated."

Can I get a witness?

If all we do is tell, we are only witnessing to cross something off the list. Guilt witnessing is not usually going to work.

When Katy Perry's song "I kissed a girl and I liked it" came out, one pastor put a sign on his marquee that read, "I kissed a girl, and I liked it, and then I went to hell."

Does that sound like it communicated to anyone? I have already established the fact that I believe in hell and sin. I'm not even going to argue the fact that a prophetic voice with a sign that says, "Bridge is out" before you drive off the cliff is sometimes needed.

My point is that most of you who picked up this book are not called to be prophets, but 100% of you are called to be witnesses. We should be people who communicate the truth of the Good

News with the motivation of a happy customer who wants to tell their friends about the amazing deal they've just found.

So zip it and listen. Take your time. Ask questions.

Questions allow a person to own an answer, often putting it into their own words instead of merely nodding their approval as you say things (and thinking about what the Bears look like this season). Jesus once asked his disciples who the masses thought he was. He then asked, *"Who do you say I am?"* and Peter stuck his neck out and said he was the Messiah (Matthew 16:13-17). Peter grew five inches that day. Now Jesus could have announced he was the Messiah and had them all write it down in their notebooks, but Peter would never have had the opportunity to step forward and grow. This was an important step in his leadership development. And it started with a question.

Questions also allow you to find out what a person already knows so you don't insult them either way. Don't assume that they don't know anything about Jesus—or that they do. I am amazed by how many people I meet who really have no idea. We don't live in Mayberry anymore.

Questions involve people; they draw them into the conversation.

Questions give people respect. A question says you care enough about what a person thinks to want to hear their opinion.

Questions assume that people can think for themselves.

And don't think that you have to have the answer to every question you ask or field. You won't. But part of a growing relationship is seeking to find the answers together.

"That's a good question," you could offer. "Why don't we each try and find an answer to that one and talk about it next time we get together?" Or "I'm not sure—let me get back to you on that one." I've been a minister for

30 years and have a Doctorate in Religion and there are still some stumpers for me.

I'm trying hard not to go into specifics with this book. I don't want this to be a "how to" book, because that limits your mission to my ideas. However, I feel like I need to give you some help with what is usually the biggest objection to Jesus in the 21st century.

ONLY WAY?

Okay, here's the biggy: "You Christians claim (or Jesus claims) that he is the only way to God." This seems exclusive and arrogant.

Kyle Idleman talks about a time he boarded a plane for California following a conference in Atlanta. This was pre-9/11, when things were a little looser at the airport. A friend of his from Dallas, who attended the same conference, also boarded the same plane. When my friend from California asked his friend why he wasn't going home to Dallas, he said, "What do you mean? I'm going to Dallas!" And when Kyle said this was a direct flight to California, his friend insisted, "No, no, this plane is going to Dallas." And he walked on by to his seat further back in the plane.

Now at this point, Kyle had a dilemma. The plane was either going to Dallas or going to California. They couldn't both be right.

Kyle said, "The guy sitting next to me . . . you know, he wanted to double-check . . . and he said, 'Yeah, this is going to California. Aren't you going to do something?' I said, 'Well, I told him he's on the wrong plane.' I didn't want to have further confrontation with my friend, so I told *on* him. I went over to the stewardess and I said, 'Hey, I have a friend back here. He probably shouldn't be traveling without a companion, but he's on the wrong plane. Can you take care of that?' And she said, 'Yeah, I'll take care of it.' A few minutes later, he came running down the aisle to get off that plane.

Now I ask you, is it arrogance or is it compassion to tell him that this plane will not take him where he thinks it's taking him? I think it would be a cruel joke to not tell him. Letting him land in California—THAT would be arrogant.

Again, I'm not suggesting that we put up a billboard that says, "I'm on the wrong plane and I like it, and I'm going to hell."

Our motivation is to save them, not to scold them. Maybe you can just use Kyle's story?

If I do love this person, if I have connected with him and served him, at some point it's going to be important for him to know that all roads don't lead to heaven—that when Jesus said, *"I am the way and the truth and the life. No one comes to the Father except through me"* (John 14:6 NIV), he wasn't being exclusive, he was just telling us where the plane is heading.

Lee Strobel points out that under our Constitution all religions are equally protected. That's a good thing and a great freedom, but many people assume that means all religions are equally valid.

Ravi Zacharias put it this way: "Truth by definition excludes that which contradicts it."[20] All religions have exclusive claims on the truth, so they can't all be true.

But it's not exclusive. I've seen exclusive. I've played golf at country clubs that are still closed to women, for crying out loud! That's exclusive. Christianity is open to everyone and it's *free*. I don't think you can call that a country club. Three times in the Bible it says *"Everyone who calls on the name of the Lord will be saved"* (Joel 2:32, Acts 2:21, Romans 10:13). Anyone and everyone.

The truth of the matter is this: Jesus is the only way, not because God is being exclusive but because NO OTHER WAY WILL WORK. No other way will save us. That's not arrogance, that's not exclusivity; that's the truth.

God knows there is no path that is going to get us to him—he must come to us, and he did exactly that.

Our sin will always hold us back, always keep us from God, and nothing else can pay for our sin except the substitute of Jesus Christ. No other way will solve the problem. God's forgiveness and grace is the only solution, and we have to make it known. Without Jesus, this plane is not going anywhere but down.

Do you really think God would have allowed his Son to die on the cross if there was any other way? What kind of God would that be?

BONO TALKS ABOUT KARMA AND GRACE

I'm going to close out this chapter with an excerpt from a Facebook interview between French author and music journalist Michka Assayas and Bono, lead singer of the Irish rock group, U2. Bono may not be your favorite example of a Christian trying to live his faith. That doesn't matter. This answer is amazing and you need to hear it. Besides some pretty solid witnessing, Bono gives us a great example of how to talk about spiritual things in a secular context. As you read this, look for the following:

- His honest embracing of his own sin nature.
- His humility.
- His respect for the other person (he doesn't make any point at the interviewer's expense or put him down for what he believes).
- His ability to incorporate other philosophies and religions without having to be threatened by them or prove them wrong.
- His use of humor, especially at his own expense.
- His ability to reason.
- He's not pushy. He lays out the truth for consideration and leaves it there. He's not going for the jugular.

- He doesn't reduce any of the truth, nor is he ashamed of the gospel in any way. The gospel, in all its power, is here for all to see.

Bono: *The thing that keeps me on my knees is the difference between Grace and Karma. I really believe we've moved out of the realm of Karma into one of Grace.*

Assayas: *I haven't heard you talk about that.*

Bono: *You see, at the center of all religions is the idea of Karma. You know, what you put out comes back to you: an eye for an eye, a tooth for a tooth, or in physics—in physical laws—every action is met by an equal or an opposite one. It's clear to me that Karma is at the very heart of the universe. I'm absolutely sure of it. And yet, along comes this idea called Grace. Grace defies reason and logic. Love interrupts, if you like, the consequences of your actions, which in my case is very good news indeed, because I've done a lot of stupid stuff.*

Assayas: *I'd be interested to hear that.*

Bono: *That's between me and God. But I'd be in big trouble if Karma was going to finally be my judge. I'd be in deep s---. It doesn't excuse my mistakes, but I'm holding out for Grace. I'm holding out that Jesus took my sins onto the Cross, because I know who I am, and I hope I don't have to depend on my own religiosity.*

Assayas: *The Son of God who takes away the sins of the world. I wish I could believe in that.*

Bono: *But I love the idea of the Sacrificial Lamb. I love the idea that God says: Look, you cretins, there are certain results to the way we are, to selfishness, and there's a mortality as part of your very sinful nature, and, let's face it, you're not living a very good life, are you? There are consequences to actions. The point of the*

death of Christ is that Christ took on the sins of the world,
so that what we put out did not come back to us, and that
our sinful nature does not reap the obvious death. That's the
point. It should keep us humbled . . . It's not our own good
works that get us through the gates of heaven.

Assayas: *That's a great idea, no denying it. Such great hope*
is wonderful, even though it's close to lunacy, in my view.
Christ has his rank among the world's great thinkers. But
Son of God, isn't that far-fetched?

Bono: *No, it's not far-fetched to me. Look, the secular*
response to the Christ story always goes like this: he was
a great prophet, obviously a very interesting guy, had a
lot to say along the lines of other great prophets, be they
Elijah, Muhammad, Buddha, or Confucius. But actually
Christ doesn't allow you that. He doesn't let you off that
hook. Christ says: No. I'm not saying I'm a teacher, don't
call me teacher. I'm not saying I'm a prophet. I'm saying:
"I'm the Messiah." I'm saying: "I am God incarnate." And
people say: No, no, please, just be a prophet. A prophet, we
can take. You're a bit eccentric. We've had John the Baptist
eating locusts and wild honey, we can handle that. But don't
mention the "M" word! Because, you know, we're gonna
have to crucify you. And he goes: No, no. I know you're
expecting me to come back with an army, and set you free
from these creeps, but actually I am the Messiah. At this
point, everyone starts staring at their shoes, and says: Oh,
man, he's gonna keep saying this. So what you're left with is:
either Christ was who He said He was—the Messiah—or a
complete nutcase.[21]

My goal here is not to load you up with answers to all the
objections of Christianity. We just want to get to the point
where we can sit down across the table from people with whom

we've earned a right to share (witness). I just wanted to give you some simple approaches to this most basic question. For the most part, your conversations should be around your story.

I think Paul Young, author of the best-selling allegory *The Shack*, has what I think is the best answer I've heard yet to the perennial "all paths" question. "No, most roads don't lead anywhere," he writes, "but God will go down any road to find you."[22]

I like that approach the best. This is never about exclusivity. It's always about the love of the Father in heaven who wants us back in his home more than anything else in the world. I can give witness to that.

GROW

CHAPTER 13

THE GREAT OMISSION

I am one of those weird guys who like to tinker with DIY (Do It Yourself). My day job is a "mind" job and it's hard to see what you're getting done at the end of the day. Sometimes I just need to make something, or mow something, or paint something, so I can see that my life is making a difference in the cosmos. That, and I have ADHD. I know I'm weird and most guys reading this are going to hate me, but my wife doesn't have a "honey-do" list. I have a "honey-what-do-you-want-me-to-do" list.

The problem is that I'm not exactly the calculating sort. "Instructions! I don't need no stinking instructions." If there isn't a hardware store nearby, I'm going to be in trouble (and something in our house will be broken).

I know I'm not alone in this, some of you reading will understand. I want to see the results of something. I want to check something off a list. I want to look back and say, "I did that."

So far, our mission looks like a checklist, and checklists are great.

Connect—Had the neighbors over last weekend. Serve—We're bringing a meal to the family who just lost a grandparent. Share— That co-worker and I are having lunch again next week, and I'm trying to work up the nerve. *Check.*

And now . . . GROW. Grow? Tim, that's not very measurable. How am I supposed to put that on a checklist? That sounds like something that takes a long time. Also, I thought this was a book about "going"? What does "grow" have to do with the Great Commission?

Everything. Let me explain.

There has been a huge misunderstanding in Christianity and church history that needs to be corrected.

Evangelicals for the last hundred years have been—true to their name—all about evangelizing. And evangelizing has been about getting people saved. So huge amounts of time, money and energy have been poured into spreading the gospel of Jesus Christ so that people all over the world could hear that Christ died for them, forgave their sins, and wants them to have eternal life with him. It's been John 3:16 all the way. So we've got John 3:16 churches all over America (and the world) full of converts who are glad to be saved but not sure what to do with themselves while waiting for that eternal life that was promised in John 3:16.

Now, as usually happens when the pendulum has swung so far in one direction, there is a movement to swing it back. Somewhere around the middle of the last half of the twentieth century, a new concept was introduced to the church, and that was the idea of discipleship, sometimes called spiritual growth. Obviously we've got to pay some attention to all these born-again Christians in church. If they are newborns, we can't expect to leave them in the pediatric ward forever.

So there gradually came to be two things that happened in your spiritual journey. One was to be saved, the other was to grow deeper in your faith. (Precisely why we have to have a "Grow" section in this book, because we still think this way.)

This two-stage spiritual growth development is so prevalent in our thinking that we have built a complex system of spiritual language and spiritual practice around these two areas.

If you're like me and grew up going to church camps or crusades, you probably remember having invitations at the end of the week, and you basically had two options: either you came forward to "make a first-time decision to accept Christ as your personal Savior," or you came forward to "rededicate your life to Christ."

Of course, the first one is the one we're really looking for. We hardly even count the other one, because Freddie rededicated his life last summer and then spent all year copying off of my homework. It could be one of a hundred times a person will rededicate his life to Christ with little or no lasting results (maybe because we are doing a bad job teaching what it means to actually follow Christ).

Or another way we talk is about the difference is separating accepting Christ as Savior and accepting him as Lord. "Savior" comes first; "Lord" comes later. Apparently you can get your Get Out Of Jail Free card and your ticket to heaven without encountering the Lord of the Starfields and Ruler of the Universe or falling down at his feet. (I wonder what Jesus thinks of this? As far as I know he's always been Lord. If someone didn't accept him as Lord, you have to wonder who it was they thought they were accepting? You can see how ridiculous this division has become and how it skews our thinking about the Lord, ourselves, sin, forgiveness . . . everything spiritual.)

Evangelism and discipleship are concepts that were never two things in the mind of Christ and should never have been in ours.

It's like peanut butter without the jelly.

What's more, we've made them weirdly conditional. Salvation is required. Discipleship is optional. It's kind of like extra credit. Yeah, that's it—it's extra credit. It's for those people who want to go deeper in their faith. When we disciple in our born-again, John 3:16 churches, we don't disciple everyone. Just the ones who are "ready for it."

What do we even call them? Members? What is a member? Jesus only knows about disciples.

Let me say it again: JESUS. ONLY. KNOWS. ABOUT. DISCIPLES. HE DOESN'T HAVE ANY OTHER OPTION IN MIND.

"If any man come after me, let him take up his membership and follow me"?

I don't think so.

As far as Jesus is concerned, salvation without discipleship is a stunted form of spirituality. It doesn't really exist. That might sound a little harsh, but I don't know of any other way to look at this. Discipleship is not an option. Discipleship is proof of evangelism. If there are no disciples in the next generation, we can come to only one conclusion as to what happened: no one was saved in this one.

Jesus didn't even bother with making converts. He skipped that step and went right to making disciples—assuming that in order to be disciples, you would of course have to be saved first. It's the great omission of the Great Commission, and we've missed it for the last hundred years.

Is it any wonder that every assessment of American religion comes up with the same conclusion today—we have more Christians than ever before, experiencing a shallower, less significant faith than ever recorded?

The question that should be blaring from the pages of this book right now is this: If you're not a disciple—if your life hasn't been completely altered in every area by Jesus Christ, if you aren't following him with every step you take—who are you, and what are you doing?

Jesus called us to be, and to make, disciples.

Our mission can't be measured by the number of people who receive Christ at a crusade or church service; it's not even measured by how many join a church, "but in the effectiveness with which the work continues in the next generation."[23] That's long-term evangelism, and it's a perspective that is outlined well in Robert Coleman's classic work from the 1960's, *Master Plan of Evangelism.*

I love that Coleman chose that title for a book that is really about discipleship. He takes a whole book to build the case that true evangelism creates full-time followers of Christ—disciples into the next generation. I couldn't agree more.

RE-THINKING SPIRITUAL GROWTH

So hold on—before you go putting your definition of discipleship into my book—let me explain what growth isn't. If you grew up in church, the word 'discipleship' might conjure up all kinds of bad memories about deathly boring Sunday School classes or Bible Olympics. Perhaps it makes you think of grumpy grandmas with Flannelgraphs (or, if you were lucky, a really sweet grandma who brought cookies to class—God bless those sweet grandmas!).

A young man in our congregation went to a Bible college and worked for a semester calling alumni to request donations for scholarships. He was used to dealing with grouchy people—after all, no one really likes being hit up for money, even if you are trying to send future kids to Bible college. He had a particularly bad experience one night when he called an 80-year-old woman— we'll call her Bertha.

Bertha griped at him throughout the entire phone call, but her final question really took the cake. She asked him with anger in her voice, "Young man, can you quote me one sentence from the book of Ezekiel?"

This young man (who, by the way, is an incredibly good guy who loves God) could think of nothing to say, being put on the spot like that. Bertha ended smugly with, "That's what I thought!"— as though passing some final judgment on this sub-par Bible college—and hung up the phone.

Friends, that's not discipleship. Spiritual growth is not memorizing Bible verses so you can spout them off to impress people. Growth is not about who is the best at following the rules and not sinning. The Pharisees were great at that and yet didn't even show up on Jesus' spiritual growth continuum.

Discipleship/Growth is simply *becoming more like Jesus.*

That's it. Jesus told his disciples in Luke 6:40 (NIV) that *"everyone who is fully trained will be like their teacher."*

This is our goal. So we connect like Jesus, we serve like Jesus, we share like Jesus and we grow to be more like Jesus every day.

How many one-sided relationships have you had that are still healthy and thriving? How many marriages survive without both spouses making an effort to communicate and continue to get to know each other?

God knows you intimately, but you and I have only experienced the tip of the iceberg. There is so much to be learned, seen, and explored of who God is. There is so much wisdom to be gained from the stories that are recorded in the Bible. The truth found in Scripture will fix our perspective, correct our assumptions, and make us love God even more.

Your word is a lamp for my feet, a light on my path (Psalm 119:105 NIV).

How can we follow Jesus on mission if we don't know where we're going?

No one serving as a soldier gets entangled in civilian affairs, but rather tries to please his commanding officer (2 Timothy 2:4 NIV).

FROM TRAINEE TO TRAINER
There's even more reason to grow if we're going to be effective agents. Paul talks about how easy it is for shallow Christians to be pulled off course.

Then we will no longer be infants, tossed back and forth by the waves, and blown here and there by every wind of teaching and by the cunning and craftiness of people in their deceitful scheming. Instead, speaking the truth in love, we will grow to become in every respect the mature body of him who is the head, that is, Christ. From him the whole body, joined and held together by every supporting ligament, grows and builds itself up in love, as each part does its work (Ephesians 4:14-16 NIV).

I'm not saying that if you are a new believer, you don't have a mission. Please don't misunderstand me. You are actually more connected to the people you need to help. We are all on mission from the second we sign up with Jesus. The disciples were "disciples" from the moment they dropped their nets and started following.

Being an "infant" also has nothing to do with the amount of time you've been following Jesus; some people jump in the deep end from the get-go, and some people have been in the kiddie pool for years. But the more you train and grow, the more effective you will be.

Let's go back to the home analogy. We start in the backyard with *Connect*. We bring some people into our home to be family by *Serving*. Some of these—or maybe some guy on a plane—we invite to the table to *Share* in spiritual discussions.

Here is where many churches and programs stop short. If this is as far as we get, we have done nothing but create a house full of people who depend on us to be fed.

At some point, if we don't teach them how to cook for themselves, they will never leave (some of you with adult children at home are saying "Amen" right now, aren't you?)

Grow is about teaching them to learn to cook and feed themselves so they will someday soon be able to take someone else through the same disciple-making process. I remember when my wife taught my young daughter how to make macaroni and cheese (from the box). She couldn't wait to make it for her friends and show them how to do it.

Do you know what that's called? Making disciples.

Jesus told us to make disciples! Our mission is to take others with us – on mission. So they can take others on mission to take others on mission.

Here is the wonderful part of this plan. The great thing about this is that you will never grow more in your faith than when you are leading someone else in faith. You never learn more than when you teach.

The people God put in your mission-path are going to ask you questions that you won't think about on your own. They will challenge you in areas of your life that you won't see on your own. That's why we do this in community. Read on.

CHAPTER 14

GUESS WHO'S COMING TO DINNER?

We had a word for community when I was growing up. *Fellowship.* It's a good word, a biblical word, but one that has been watered down through the years. When I was growing up we had fellowship dinners—in essence, good old-fashioned southern potlucks. You'd put out the 8-foot tables end to end and everyone pitched in. You could eat the meatloaf that was always there, or you could stick your spoon in the crock pot someone had plugged into a long, dangerous extension chord, and see how lucky you were coming out of the pot. There was always 3 bean salad. Plenty of Jell-O® and Rice Krispy® treats, and of course the proverbial bucket of KFC® from someone who didn't have time to actually cook (and this was also the most popular, so as a preacher's kid I learned early the art of getting to the front of the line).

The adults would stand around the church basement afterwards with coffee cups in their hands, the kids would play four square or ping pong in the youth room, or hide under the pews, or play football on the front lawn in the summer.

It was indeed fellowship, but only at a surface level. To say it added to anyone's spiritual growth would have been an overstatement.

In at least one case, it actually was a deterrent to spiritual growth for me. This is just a funny story that has nothing to do with my point, except that it's my most vivid memory of a "fellowship" dinner from my childhood. In our church in Oklahoma there was a miserly woman who was at least one taco short of a combination plate, if you know what I mean. She wouldn't eat all weekend if we were having a potluck. Then she would proceed to eat more than an NFL linebacker at the dinner, more than I could put down as a teenage boy. Afterwards, she would stuff her purse and jacket with anything she could possibly take home. She was a potluck-lifter. A fellowship kleptomaniac. I'm pretty sure she never brought anything either, unless it was something she still had left from last month's dinner.

Well, one day one of the other older ladies finally took Klepto-Christian to task and told her that this restaurant didn't allow doggie bags. And that's when the fight started. Literally. I want to sit by Jesus and watch the rerun of this one in heaven some day. I imagine him looking down at the "fellowship" dinner at a "Christian" church...while two old ladies are literally in a cage match wrestling on the floor. Sarah Lee® and Oreos® flying everywhere.

I wonder if there were any first timers there that Sunday afternoon . . .

We've already talked about the importance of meals to this process of mission (this one notwithstanding). But there was a lot more to fellowship than meatloaf. The Greek word for it is *koinonia*, which implies a sense of communion and intimacy that goes way further than a cup of coffee and NFL discussion.

It is koinonia that is imperative to mission and to growth. This happens when believers come together with Jesus in their midst and seek honest, open relationships. So hear me now—if you're not in community/fellowship/koinonia right now, you need to be if you're going to be On Mission.

I'm talking about people at various stages of growth, on different legs of their mission, living in community together to help each other change the world! Like this . . .

> *All the believers were together and had everything in common.*
> *They sold property and possessions to give to anyone who had need.*
> *Every day they continued to meet together in the temple courts.*
> *They broke bread in their homes and ate together with glad and*
> *sincere hearts, praising God and enjoying the favor of all the people.*
> *And the Lord added to their number daily those who were being*
> *saved* (Acts 2:44-47 NIV).

Never was the mission clearer and purer than at the very beginning.

Bob Russell said once, "The early church exploded in growth because the people loved being together. When you get a group of people together who genuinely believe something and who really enjoy each other, it's such a contagious atmosphere that you can't keep people away from it."[24]

The primary reason to meet regularly with other Christians is not to learn more biblical information. It's not to develop great friends. It's not even accountability. It is connectedness. Belonging to a small group of believers in a close and transparent relationship ties you to the people and information you will need when a need-to-grow or need-to-know crisis shows up.

Hebrews puts it this way: *And let us consider how we may spur one another on toward love and good deeds, not giving up meeting together, as some are in the habit of doing, but encouraging one another—and all the more as you see the Day approaching* (Hebrews 10:24-25 NIV).

Close and transparent relationships allow for a healthy peer pressure to do its good work. We all conform to those around us. Sermons can be a powerful catalyst for spiritual insight and growth (I wouldn't waste my time preparing and presenting sermons on a weekly basis if I didn't believe that!). But we would be kidding ourselves if we believed that sermons alone could produce long-term, life-changing spirituality.

Here's the analogy again. We establish relationships in the backyard—Connect. We invite them into our home—Serve. We invite them to sit at the kitchen table—Share. We help them learn to cook for themselves—Grow. *And we're never in the kitchen alone.*

THE CHURCH MELTING POT

Hang on a second, Tim—you're telling me that I need healthy peer pressure and community, *and* that I should be hanging around with people who don't know God? How does that work?

Let's break this down for a minute. There are a couple of things I want to address.

First—please identify your specific areas of weakness. If you are a recovering alcoholic, please don't do your outreach in a bar. If your marriage is on the rocks, don't go seeking out people of the opposite sex to "mentor" (and please go get counseling). If you struggle with your finances or materialism, don't have your coffee date at the mall.

When Jesus first sent his disciples out on assignment, he said, *"I am sending you out like sheep among wolves. Therefore be as shrewd as snakes and as innocent as doves"* (Matthew 10:16 NIV). Please be smart about your areas of temptation and *run from them.*

You are not Jesus (newsflash). Neither am I. There are some people who are far from God that someone else is going to have to help. They could wreck my marriage or my life if I'm around them. You will have to be like a sheep among wolves. Read—"be careful."

But even if you aren't the one to help them, this idea of being like Jesus is about getting rid of the pride in our hearts that gives us an "us-them" mentality towards certain sins. It's probably not *your* specific area of temptation that is keeping you from reaching out to a particular person— it's a lot more likely to be concern of what others will think or the fact that you're a lot more comfortable in your church bubble.

I can spend all night in a bar without any temptation to get drunk. Maybe you can't. Be shrewd as snakes (don't walk straight into a situation you know will be a snare for you) and innocent as doves (ask God to reveal and remove pride from your heart and give you compassion for others).

Second—don't abandon your friends who are mature believers. You need them!

If you're in three church groups and serve at church two other days of the week, maybe you *do* need to drop something to make space for non-Christians in your life. But I'm not asking you to drop your Christian friends.

Again—Jesus modeled this by spending most of his time with his 12 closest "Christian" (so to speak) friends and by eating with "sinners."

You need both. You need to be speaking into someone else's life, and you need someone mature speaking into your life.

Even the Lone Ranger had Tonto (and Silver). The beauty of this mission plan is that as you go on mission and connect and serve and share, as soon as a person decides to follow Jesus, they have an automatic growth group—YOURS—to hang out with. Ideally, the lines between these groups would eventually start to blur as new Christians and honestly seeking non-Christians come join the Jesus family.

I'm guessing the members of your Christian community – be that a small group, Bible Study, Sunday School class, or even your flesh and blood family – probably need a little encouragement to be around some of the "non-healthy people Jesus came to help" (Mark 2:17).

But our *koinonia* should look pretty diverse. Church is nothing if not a big melting pot of extremely different people. I love Matt Chandler's depiction of the first converts of the church of Philippi—a wealthy fashionista entrepreneur, a hyper-emotional demon-possessed slave girl, and a blue-collar jailer with an identity completely defined by his job.[255]

What happens when people who are all the same get together and start talking? *Nothing.* Everyone just affirms each other's already-formed opinions. No one is challenged, no one grows. So embrace the melting pot! God gave us the church to be a place where we all belong, regardless of background, politics, socio-economic status, or baseball affiliations.

We need people around us who really want to know how we are—and who we can trust with the truth. People who know us well enough that when they speak into our life, it fits our reality, not our image.

Mindy Caliguire is the founder of the spiritual formation ministry Soul Care. Here's what she had to say when I asked her recently about this link between relationships and spiritual growth:

> *I think one of the most critical elements of spiritual formation or spiritual development are the same kinds of relationships that actually drew us into faith.*
>
> *We don't end those once we become a believer. We need those kinds of relationships to run this race together and become the kinds of people that honor God naturally. We must get away from this very independent version of spiritual formation or development. It's a big relational deal. God's a relational god. We are relational humans made in His likeness. We desperately need each other to grow.*
>
> *Sometimes you're in a place where you might be a little further along in your journey, and you think, "Wow...I know all the mistakes I've made." You have something to offer by virtue of your friendship with somebody who's just a little ways up the road. You can help them. You can sit around a table; ask them how they're doing. Ask them how their life with God is going. Don't be weird and invasive, but just ask them how they're doing. How can you be a prayer person for them? See what will unfold, but keep in mind that for all of us to grow, for all of us to become who we're going to become, it's going to happen in the context of community.*

You also might be somebody who's feeling a little stuck. You came to faith. You had this season of intensity, and now it just doesn't feel that same way. I would challenge you to look around. Who is running this race with you? And if you don't see anyone yet who is that person alongside you, maybe look around on a Sunday morning. Who else is around? Is there somebody you have natural business relationships with? Or community relationships with that you respect? You see that they're a little bit further down the road. Don't wig them out and ask them to do something major, like for the next 20 years to be your mentor. Just say, "Hey, can I buy you a cup of coffee and ask you about your journey?"

What could open up for you might be one of the most powerful things for your own spiritual growth. Our growth as believers is essential to the rest of the great commission being fulfilled because it's only those people who are deeply alive to God who are that compelling witness out there in the world. Find those people that you can run your race with so that you can experience the kind of growth and transformation that God has for you, and you get more into the adventure of helping others in their journey as well.

Philippians 1:27 (NLT): *I will know that you are standing together with one spirit and one purpose, fighting together for the faith, which is the Good News.*

Philippians 1:5 (NLT): *. . . you have been my partners in spreading the Good News about Christ.*

Being discipled in the close fellowship of transparent relationships, leaving room for the real Jesus to show up in our midst, is the most powerful model for growth there is.

One more thing. There is a Jewish tradition that if someone asks to come to dinner, they can't be refused. That's why when Jesus invited himself to Zack's place, Zacheaus had to accept him. (I bet Jesus made good use of that tradition, given that he was homeless.)

I think we should adopt this tradition as well. When anyone wants to join our fellowship, let him in. This isn't a country club. And if we welcome anyone, we will guarantee that our own welcome continues. Once you let Jesus in, you've got to let all his friends in too, and some of them are pretty messy. That's the problem with Jesus. He never says no.

CHAPTER 15

LESSONS IN SAILING

Therefore let us move beyond the elementary teachings about Christ and be taken forward to maturity (Hebrews 6:1 NIV).

Let's go back to this idea of leaving the pediatric ward. Our mission will be thwarted if we don't grow up—you don't want kindergartners running the nursery. But maturity? Holiness? Yikes! When will I ever get there?

When I was younger, verses like this one from Matthew used to really freak me out: *"Be perfect, therefore, as your heavenly Father is perfect"* (Matthew 5:48 NIV). To a kid who has only perfected the art of getting in scrapes and terrorizing his younger sister, this sounds like a death sentence. You have got to be kidding me. Does being perfect include never getting grass stains on your Levis? If so, I am doomed to the fiery flames.

I hope we're all on the same page by now and understand that nothing but Jesus' sacrifice is what yanks us out of hell by the scruff of our necks. And yet . . . here we are, rubbing our necks, left to grapple with commands like this. Grow up. Be holy.

How? Is it something we do, or is it something only God can do— or is it somehow, weirdly, both?

On one hand, there are those Chuck Norris Christians who are determined to make themselves holy. They study their Bibles in hopes of taking down any unsuspecting Jehovah's Witnesses who show up at their doorstep on Saturday morning. For them, the church becomes a place of contest to see who is the most holy, who has memorized the most Bible verses (to have the last word), who has witnessed to the most people, who has the most regular quiet time, and who has prayed the most. Their definition of "disciple" includes all the "taking up your cross," and "laying down your life" verses.

At the other extreme, there are Christians who object to any call for effort or discipline because they think that human effort is opposed to grace. Their definition of disciple includes the "easy yoke" and "whoever believes" verses.

So what does a disciple look like? And who's responsible—us or God?

The answer is yes.

Think about the differences between a motorboat and a sailboat. In a motorboat, I'm in control. I start the engine, control the speed, and go wherever I want. Sailing is different. When I'm sailing, I'm not passive—I have a role to play—I hoist the sails and steer with the rudder, but I am utterly dependent on the wind. There's no room for believing I'm in control, because if the wind doesn't blow, I'm dead in the water. When the wind does blow, on the other hand, amazing things can happen.

A disciple is a sailor.

The word for wind is the same as the word for Spirit both in Hebrew and in Greek. Jesus says the wind blows wherever it chooses. We hear the sound, but we don't know where it comes from, and we don't know where it goes. It's free and formidable, way beyond our control. The transforming work of the Holy Spirit is powerful and mysterious. We can't control or manufacture it. It's not about us coming up with a program with predictable results we control. On the other hand, we're not passive. Our job is to discern where the wind of the Spirit is blowing and grab the rope and hoist the sail.

Ultimately, I believe in God's sovereignty—meaning that God is in control over everything. I believe God is big and strong and good enough to do whatever he wants with me and through me. This is why we don't need to achieve some level of growth before we start helping others down the path of discipleship and their mission. We do not need to achieve some level of maturity for God to use us. We will be more effective if we allow him to help us grow and know him on a deeper level, but ultimately God is only using me because he is good. He knows how much joy my life will have when I'm in the boat with him, leading others to catch the same wind.

So we work together to catch the wind of the Spirit and go places we could not have imagined.

But what about that maturity thing?

If we did a poll, I bet just about all of us would say that a gap exists between the people God made us to be and the people we currently are. We live in that tension, and a problem arises when we think it's up to us to close the gap.

You hear about someone who gets up at four o'clock in the morning to pray, and you feel guilty because you think you don't pray enough, and you resolve to do that, too, even though you are not a morning person, even though at four o'clock in the morning you are dazed and confused and grumpy and groggy, and nobody wants to be around you . . . even Jesus!

But you think—well, that is hard and exhausting and miserable, and I don't like doing it, so it must be God's will for my life. It must be spiritual. It must be good for me. (Kind of like health food, right? The worse it tastes, the better it must be for me. Kale— enough said.) And you try to do it, and maybe for a few days or weeks or even a month you pull something off, but eventually you stop, and then you feel more guilt because you stopped. Then when the guilt gets high enough, you start trying something else, and that frustrating cycle sets in again. Guilt—start to do something—doesn't work—get tired—stop doing it—guilt builds back up and you start back at the top. This is tiring for the soul. Is this what it takes to grow as a disciple?

Please hear the Apostle Paul on this one:

Oh, foolish Galatians! Who has cast an evil spell on you? For the meaning of Jesus Christ's death was made as clear to you as if you had seen a picture of his death on the cross. Let me ask you this one question: Did you receive the Holy Spirit by obeying the law of Moses? Of course not! You received the Spirit because you believed the message you heard about Christ. How foolish can you be? After starting your Christian lives in the Spirit, why are you now trying to become perfect by your own human effort? (Galatians 3:1-3 NLT)

Can I bridge this gap through human effort? Not a chance. Plenty of people are trying . . . I've tried myself more often than I'd care to admit. *Well, I got saved by grace, but then I guess I have to live by human effort. I guess I have to get from A to Z by muscling it out.*

No. Just as you got saved by grace, so you are invited to live by grace, and this is the only way real transformation happens. Everything God does for us is grace—meaning, it's given freely based on his love, and we can't do anything to earn it.

When you first come to God, you may experience grace primarily as forgiveness, and of course, grace is forgiveness, but it's more than that. God was a gracious God before anybody ever sinned. Creation itself was an act of grace.

God's plan is for you to live every day by grace, to learn to run on grace, to wake up in grace, and to receive life and energy as a gift from him.

Sometimes we think that people who are sinners need grace but saints don't anymore. Nothing could be further from the truth.

Dallas Willard says, "Saints burn way more grace than sinners ever could."[26] Saints run on grace. It is like rocket fuel. It's like food. Grace is more than something you need when you sin; it's what we are intended to live on all the time. Grace is the generosity of God, and once I become a Christian, I experience it now primarily as power, to do what I otherwise could not do.

It's the wind filling our sails.

So what do *we* do?

We train.

There is a big difference between *trying* and *training*.

Do you not know that in a race all the runners run, but only one gets the prize? Run in such a way as to get the prize. Everyone who competes in the games goes into strict training. They do it to get a crown that will not last, but we do it (go into strict training) to get a crown that will last forever, to experience goodness that cannot be stopped. Therefore, I do not run like a man running aimlessly. I do not fight like a man beating the air. No, I beat my body and make it my slave so that after I preach to others, I myself will not be disqualified for the prize (1 Corinthians 9:24-27 NIV).

How many people could go outside today and run every step of a marathon right now? (If you're reading this and you could, just imagine along with the rest of us mere mortals.) Most of us couldn't. Even if we tried *really, really, really* hard.

But most of us COULD run a marathon eventually, if we really wanted to and have been blessed with healthy limbs. How? We would train, of course!

To train means to arrange your life around those activities that enable you to someday accomplish what you cannot do now. Training is an athlete putting in hours at the gym and on the field. Training is a musician logging hours of scales and warm-ups to the tick of the metronome. Training is reading up on leadership books before you go for that promotion at work, or diligently completing practice tests before taking your ACT.

Is there a difference between the training and trying? Absolutely. They might both involve you getting up early. They will both involve pushing yourself to do some things that are good for you. The difference is the motivation. If I think I need to get up early to read my Bible to make God happy, it will be drudgery. If I decide to read my Bible every day (whenever it works for me) because I realize how much good it does in my life, how much better I am as a person, how it helps infuse my day with the Spirit of God—it will become a joy.

When we open up our Bibles, we allow the truth about God's character to imprint itself on our minds. In our usually one-sided dialogue with God, it gives us the chance to shut up and listen to what he might want to say to us. When we tithe regularly or give to a charity or sponsor a child, when we loosen our tight grip on money, God can teach us about his faithfulness and make us people who love others more than money. When we take the time to be still and pray, we train our minds to remember that he is in control and in our midst.

I'm a person who exercises regularly, and sleeps regularly, and eats pretty well. When I don't do those things, I feel terrible. I feel sluggish and ill-equipped to tackle my day. God created my body to move more than it does in front of a computer all day. My body is designed to eat food that comes from plants, not a processing-plant. I need plenty of rest. It's how I was made. Your spiritual body is the same.

Anything you do for training should make you feel better. And everyone is different. Maybe you like kale. I can't stand it. People tell me I need to know how to buy it or cook it—but it's just a nasty weed and I'm not going to eat it. Or brussel sprouts. OK? But I am going to eat spinach because I like spinach (I grew up on Popeye). I am cutting a lot of gluten out of my diet. White processed sugar and flour—no big deal. When I realize what those things do to my body, I'm willing to let it go. But I will not be eating kale—did I make myself clear?

Gary Thomas wrote a very helpful book on the subject called "Sacred Pathways: Discover your soul's path to God." In it he talks about the multiple ways people find spiritual health and growth and maturity.[27] It's not a cookie cutter approach. At my health club they have one side devoted to CrossFit®, a bunch of rooms for the Zumba®/kickboxing/pilates classes, a section of free weights, a section of machines, and a room devoted to cardio with treadmills, ellipticals, and stair climbing machines, and a room for a spinning class (which is a fancy word for riding a bike that goes nowhere).

The point is that everyone trains differently. But everyone trains.

This is how we harness the wind. This is how we handle the boat. It will probably feel clumsy at first, if you aren't accustomed to it, but don't give up. Get some experienced sailors around you to show you the ropes. There is no limit to what God can do through you.

Some days it may not work. Some days it may feel hard to go to the spiritual gym, just like it does the real one. In the movie *Karate Kid*, the young student must go through a long period of activities that in his mind have nothing to do with karate. In fact, you might remember that he thinks his master is taking advantage of him by making him wax his car, paint his fence and sand and finish his floors. It's not until he has done all this that he sees how these skills have prepared him to do karate.[28] Perseverance pays off just as it does with the spiritual disciplines of reading the Bible, praying, giving, and spending time with other believers.

There will come a day at work when God says: "Show me grace instead of ambition," a day in your marriage when God says: "Show me gentleness instead of anger," a day when you don't get what you think you deserve when God says: "Show me contentment instead of greed," a day when someone hurts you when God says: "Show me mercy instead of vengeance," and you will know what to do. You will know how. By persisting through the detours and waiting, by persevering through all the in-between times, by incorporating all these strange disciplines of faith, you will discover that you have been transformed.

FORGET WHAT IS BEHIND

Not that I have already obtained all this, or have already been made perfect, but I press on to take hold of that for which Christ Jesus took hold of me. Brothers, I do not consider myself yet to have taken hold of it. But one thing I do: Forgetting what is behind and straining toward what is ahead, I press on toward the goal to win the prize for which God has called me heavenward in Christ Jesus (Philippians 3:12-14 NIV).

First I have to forget what is behind me. We tend to think of forgetting as a bad thing, as something we shouldn't do. But forgetting can be good! Paul urges us to keep going and to forget what is behind. Paul allows neither his failures nor his successes to keep him trapped in yesterday.

Transformation is a process. Don't give up. It's not a sprint, it's a marathon. Forget what is behind and reach for what is ahead. Eventually your efforts will become habits, and your habits, character. Have you ever met a person who has walked with Jesus for a really, really long time? I'm fortunate to have examples in both my parents and my wife's parents— these are the kinds of people who radiate with God's love. It gives me hope that all of this training really does pay off.

The Bible calls the evidence of God's work in us "fruit of the Spirit"— meaning, if our sails are filled, it will produce good results that other people can see. In the same letter to the Galatians, where moments ago Paul was chastising them for trying to forge their own holiness without the Spirit's help, he gives them this encouragement: *But the fruit of the Spirit is love, joy, peace, forbearance, kindness, goodness, faithfulness, gentleness and self-control* (Galatians 5:22-23 NIV).

These are the qualities that will start to show up in our lives as evidence of our transformation.

I wish I could hit you with a magic transformation pill. I wish you could get bitten by a spider and turned into a superhero. But transformation will happen if you let it!

Ask my wife how important transformation continues to be in my life. Ask my kids. They will tell you how important my transformation is, and has been to my family, and how important it is and will be to you and yours.

Just listen to this story of transformation from a friend of mine.

> *Dear Tim,*
>
> *This is our story about how Jesus Christ delivered me and healed our marriage.*
>
> *For years I struggled with rages of anger. Twenty-five years of our marriage my wife and kids walked on eggshells. I was abusive, controlling, physical, emotional, spiritual, and mental.*
>
> *I prayed for years to be healed, had elders pray over me and anoint me with oil. Still the rages continued. I read books on anger and how to control it. None of it worked. Finally in 2003 I threw a five pound candle at my oldest son, hitting him in the arm. He called the police and I was arrested. Before this my wife wanted a divorce. I was determined not to let this happen. So I spent the night in jail. This was the best thing that ever happened to me. As I was waiting for the judge in a sardine can of a room, Jesus asked me, "Are you ready for me to take charge of your life?"*
>
> *"Yes Lord, I am."*
>
> *My wife and I separated because I was not allowed to go back to our house for 3 days. I spent the nights in a motel.*

For 2 years we were separated. I spent massive time in God's word meditating on verses he knew I needed, and he wrote on my heart and mind. Verses on love, anger, and how to forgive, and how to speak the truth in love, and how to love, and what love is. Agape love—a love that loves without expecting anything in return. This was God's love that changed my heart. In May of 2005, God brought us back together after dating for a while. We have been together since. God is so awesome.

Are you aware of having certain patterns in your life that you are unable—even unwilling to change? They seem so entrenched, so beyond your ability to do anything about. You might even see yourself walking in the same path of a parent or a grandparent and you realize this rut runs generations deep. How am I ever going to be able to overcome against these odds?

Do not be conformed any longer to the pattern of this world, but be transformed by the renewing of your mind (Romans 12:2 NIV).

Train. The word of God is full of truth with which you can renew your mind. This is not just positive thinking or a motivational weekend designed to blow us out of our ruts—this is God's word, and God's word never returns empty. It accomplishes its purpose (Isaiah 55:11).

Yes, it will take effort. Change doesn't come easy nor does it come overnight, but it comes as we purposely focus on the new truth about ourselves that Christ has won. We are loved. We are forgiven. We have his Spirit. We don't have to walk in those old patterns. We can break the pattern. There is no condemnation for those who are in Christ Jesus.

There are a lot of conflicting messages out there; there's a lot of negative reinforcement in our minds. Do nothing and you probably will keep on rattling along in the same rut. Renew your mind with God's word and his truth about yourself and you can stand down those old voices and start down a new path. It's worth it. We aren't just waiting for heaven. We are fighting a battle here.

We are on a mission. We have a gospel to live out.

And if the gospel doesn't work in our lives, how can we recommend it to anyone else?

PRAY

CHAPTER 16

TAKE ADVANTAGE OF THE UNIVERSE

At this point, you'd be tempted to think that prayer is an "add on" for me to put in this book on mission. I did struggle with it, but not because I couldn't be the guy who forgot about prayer. It's the opposite for me. Initially I listed prayer first because there is no mission without the power of God. It's his mission. He's the one giving us the self-destructing tape player in the first place. Eventually I decided to put it last, because now that you understand the mission, you know you're going to need God a lot more than he needs you. You'll know why you need to cover everything in prayer.

Prayer comes into play on this mission in a few different ways. Let's talk about the first one—prayer as a way of introducing one friend to another.

We cookout in the backyard—Connect. We invite them in—Serve. We take them to the table—Share. We show them around the kitchen—Grow. During this process, there's always got to be a place in the house where you go to be alone and talk to God. *"When you pray, go into your room, close the door and pray to your Father, who is unseen"* (Matthew 6:6 NIV). But in the same way that we let our friends into the kitchen to learn how to cook (Grow), we also need to invite them into our prayer space.

The really good news about this mission is that people are searching for God. They always have been searching for God. It has looked different throughout history and across different generations, but Blaise Pascal's "God-shaped vacuum" remains the same, and people long to fill it. What I'm saying is that this is not about selling something to someone who doesn't know if they need it. They may have had some bad experiences with their perception of God or his people, but this is their most basic human need.

We now live in a world full of people who call themselves "spiritual." It means something different every time, but at the core, it's a search for God. Remember when *The Secret* was the big deal? (Mostly because Oprah made it a big deal—I hope she likes this book— someone please give it to her.)

That was an interesting time for America, when thousands of bed-ridden individuals were exposed to the philosophy of Positive Energy and tried wishing themselves out of the flu.

The premise of *The Secret* is that the Universe has different energy frequencies that we can tap into through our thoughts. By thinking positively and imagining a certain outcome, we can will that scenario into existence.

I watched in amazement as people bought that book and subscribed to this new brand of "spirituality."

It excited me. Don't get me wrong, I didn't agree with it. I found myself saying "I do believe in fairies. I do. I do. I do believe in fairies."

What excited me is that if you can show me a person who subscribes to the Universe vending machine theory, I'll show you a person who is genuinely seeking spiritual truth. Someone who is hungry for depth, for significance.

As hostile as our country may be to Christianity as a religion, there has never been a time where people have been more open to discussing spiritual topics. I mean, honestly—back in "Leave it to Beaver" time, everyone went to church, but can you imagine discussing the deep spiritual matters with the Cleavers?

People are hungry to find meaning in their existence. Hungry for spiritual connectedness. I would venture so far as to say . . . hungry for God.

Listen to what Paul says in Romans: *For since the creation of the world God's invisible qualities—his eternal power and divine nature—have been clearly seen, being understood from what has been made, so that people are without excuse* (Romans 1:20 NIV). We see glimpses of God's divinity all around us—in sunsets, in hurricanes, in constellations, in friendship. These experiences are universal, and they point us at something larger than ourselves. They make us hungry for more of the divine.

So how do we tap into this hunger?

I challenge you to take this simple question into the boxing ring: *Is there anything you'd like me to pray for?*

I already told you to ask questions, but there are some questions that may lead to a dead-end. "Would you like to come to church?" "Would you like to join my expository Bible study on the book of Revelation?" But I am telling you, I've never heard of anyone giving a hostile response to the question, *How can I pray for you?*

Not only are people NOT hostile, but you wouldn't believe how grateful many people are to get the question. Some of your neighbors and co-workers may be wrestling through some really tough seasons, and the fact that you're willing to pray for their teenager who just got suspended or a father with Alzheimer's may really strike a chord.

Plato said, "Be kind. Everyone you meet is fighting a battle."

Let's take it a step further. Let's pray for their battle.

Our church is involved in Courtside Prayer ministries. They just go to the courthouse with a fold up table and people ready to pray. As people are coming and going, they just ask if they have need of prayer. It's a beautiful thing. At the courthouse we work with, about 25% of people stop and pray, can you imagine that? These people are heading to the courthouse because they got evicted, they're getting divorced, they have a trial. Unless you work there, you aren't usually going through that door for a good reason.

Everyone is fighting a battle. And a lot of people would really like help fighting it.

If they have nothing but a small crack in their door to faith, they will likely give it a shot. What is there to lose for them? Offering to pray doesn't insult your friend's pain. How many of us have lost loved ones only to have some well-meaning but insensitive Jesus-juker come along and say something trite? *"Well, you just need to let go and let God."* That might be answered by "How 'bout I let go with a blow to your midsection?"

Prayer doesn't do that. It's not the quick fix.

Prayer acknowledges two very important things. 1) You care about their pain; and 2) You believe in a good God who also cares about their pain. Prayer is offering to share another's burdens. Prayer is saying, "I don't want you to have to suffer through this alone, and I'm asking for peace and courage and energy for you when you feel like you can't get through the day."

Author and discipleship expert Bill Hull shared recently about a powerful experience of praying this way with a friend:

> *I spend quite a bit of time at Starbucks. It is my place I go every day to just relax for a few minutes. There is a guy there, let's just call him Ken, and Ken is an avowed atheist. He is always telling me there is not enough evidence for God. He shows me all kinds of articles and he sends things to me on the Internet about how crazy and nutty Christians are…I call him my favorite infidel. We discuss all these kinds of things at great length.*
>
> *Not long ago, his father was dying, and I asked him, "So, you're sad. You're sad about your father. He is dying. What do you think happens next?" He says, "Nothing happens next." I said, "If you thought that there could be something, would you be happy if you could know that?" He said, "Yeah, I really would." I said, "Would*

you mind if I prayed for you?" He said, "No, I guess not. It can't hurt." So I prayed for him. I put my arm around him and prayed for him and it brought tears to his eyes. From that time forward, I just started treating him as a person who needed God, who was touched by other people's love and concern, and as I have continued to dialog with him, he is getting closer and closer to admitting that possibly there might be something else.

Here's another great story—Dori Gorman and her husband were starting a church in a Chicago neighborhood, and in those early stages there wasn't much to do except pray and pray hard. They came up with this incredibly creative way to both pray *with* and pray *for* the people of their neighborhood.

My husband was sitting in a coffee shop. Sometimes in Chicago, prayer walks in the wintertime are more like "prayer sits." You sit in a coffee shop and look out the window and pray for people as they walk by because it's cold. He was sitting in a coffee shop praying and really felt burdened for the neighborhood and noticed that everyone, as they walked by, just were sort of hurry-worried, busy, and just were all looking down. He really felt this burden. How are we going to tell people about the love of Christ? I don't really want to be the guy with a bullhorn on the corner, but there are over 300,000 people in three square miles in our neighborhood—how do we tell all of them about Jesus?

He just noticed they were all looking down. I don't know if in prayer God spoke to him in "sidewalk talk." It was the weirdest thing. He came home and told it to me, the idea of chalking encouraging messages to our neighborhood as a way of pastoring the neighborhood and telling people that we were praying for them without using those words, necessarily.

I was like, "That sounds cheesy. I don't know…" But we did it, and lo and behold, it ended up being a huge way that we have really pastored our neighborhood. We've walked and prayed for people and then stopped and chalked things like, "You are loved," and "All things can be made new again," and "Maybe what you're holding onto is actually holding you back." Things like that. Great conversations have come from those chalked messages. Literally, our prayers for this neighborhood, written on the street. We haven't looked back, and great stories of people being impacted through prayer and those words have come from it.

GREAT EXPECTATIONS

Now when we talk about praying for specific situations—for healing, for restored relationships, for a job, etc.—we can't avoid talking about how God chooses to answer those prayers, and this is tricky business. We all know of situations where God miraculously intervened . . . and we all know someone godly who prayed earnestly for healing that didn't come.

For those of us who know and follow God, it's not an issue of whether God is capable. We know he is. It's not even necessarily an issue of whether we believe God hears and answers our prayers. We know he does. But experience has taught us that God doesn't always answer our prayers in the way, or at the time, we think ideal. Theoretically, most Christians are pretty okay with this—after all, his ways are not our ways and all that.

However, if we pray for someone who isn't a Christian, and it feels like God isn't answering . . . the pressure is on!

Can we just be honest and admit that we're afraid that God has bad PR skills? I'm afraid that if I pray for the illness to pass, it might not, and Jesus and I will both look like fools. Even worse—what if the person for whom I'm praying totally rejects God after the experience, because God said "no?"

I think part of this is the approach. Some churches and believers actually believe that they can tell God what to do. Jesus said to pray "Your will be done."

There is a difference. But praying in faith will never go wrong.

The Bible commands us to pray with great expectations. James 1:6-8 (NIV) says when we ask we *must believe and not doubt, because he who doubts is like a wave of the sea, blown and tossed by the wind. That person should not expect to receive anything from the Lord. Such a person is double-minded and unstable in all they do.*

And Hebrews 11:6 (NIV) says that *without faith it is impossible to please God, because anyone who comes to him must believe that he exists and that he rewards those who earnestly seek him.*

The bottom line is that we can trust God with the results. Sometimes we forget that he loves our friends and family members even more than we do. He wants his kids to come home; He wants all men to come to repentance. We can trust him to do what is best. Our job is to pray expectantly, with total confidence in our Heavenly Father.

There's a great story in Acts about a group of people who didn't pray expectantly and got a pretty good shock. Herod has just killed James, and after he sees that it gets him popularity points with the Jews, he arrests Peter, too. The church is up all night praying for Peter, and amazingly, an angel comes and busts him out of prison. Surrounded by guards, Peter slips right out of his chains and through the iron gates.

When he shows up at the house where everyone is praying for him, he's met by a servant girl named Rhoda. Rhoda is so overjoyed that she actually forgets to open the door. She runs to tell the others of Peter's arrival, and they don't believe her. They think she's been to Colorado for medicinal marijuana. Eventually

Peter's persistent knocking interrupts the conversation, and he finally gets let into the house to testify to his own safety.

Isn't this incredible? They very people who are praying for Peter accuse the girl who brings them their answer of being 'out of her mind'—they actually accuse her of insanity!

Peter's escape shouldn't have been a surprise. After all, Jesus said, *"If two of you on earth agree about anything you ask for, it will be done for you by my Father in heaven. For where two or three come together in my name, there am I with them"* (Matthew 18:19-20 NIV). Unfortunately, I think the church was probably pretty discouraged at this point. James had just been put to death in prison, which would have been a terrible blow—they probably expected the same fate for Peter.

Good thing God doesn't live up to our paltry expectations, right?

Pray boldly. And by the way—it's okay to be honest with your friends who aren't Christians. You're the witness, not the defense attorney, remember? It's okay to admit that you don't know how God might choose to work, but that you trust him to do what is best. It's okay to talk about a time when you felt like God wasn't answering your prayers. People appreciate your humility and honesty more than you could possibly imagine.

And if you're feeling a little apprehensive about praying with someone, if you're a little anxious about how a situation might turn out . . . well, the instructions remain the same.

Do not be anxious about anything, but in every situation, by prayer and petition, with thanksgiving, present your requests to God. And the peace of God, which transcends all understanding, will guard your hearts and your minds in Christ Jesus (Philippians 4:6-7 NIV).

CHAPTER 17

ACE OF HEARTS

"TALKING TO MEN FOR GOD IS A GREAT THING, BUT TALKING TO GOD FOR MEN IS GREATER STILL."

- E.M. BOUNDS

Let's talk about the human heart.

Don't freak out, I'm not about to get Disney on you. As a man who has been very outnumbered at home by X chromosomes for over 26 years, I can still tell you everything I know about the human heart in only one sentence. Are you ready for this golden nugget of wisdom? Here's what I've learned about the heart:

It's unpredictable and weird.

That was worth the whole price of the book, right? You had no idea we were going so deep.

I've had the privilege of being married to one of the most beautiful, godly women in the world for over thirty years. Thanks to her incredible parenting skills, we've raised three beautiful, godly daughters. You'd think I'd be an expert on the human heart.

Nope. The heart is a mystery to me. But there is someone who knows the human heart better than any other. The Psalms put it this way:

> From heaven the Lord looks down and sees all mankind; from his dwelling place he watches all who live on earth—he who forms the hearts of all, who considers everything they do (Psalm 33:13-15 NIV).

> You have searched me, Lord, and you know me. You know when I sit and when I rise; you perceive my thoughts from afar. You discern my going out and my lying down; you are familiar with all my ways. Before a word is on my tongue, Lord, you know it completely (Psalm 139:1-4).

There is one crucial piece left in your mission—miss it, and you definitely won't succeed.

You may be the most charming, well-spoken, good-natured person in the room. You may have a dangerous knack for manipulation. But all of the best shared meals, all of your visits to the hospital, all of your time spent brilliantly breaking down the gospel, all of the fruit of the Spirit displayed in your life cannot change another human heart.

ONLY GOD CAN CHANGE A HUMAN HEART.

The most loving thing you can do for another person is pray for him.

A lot of people ask Denise and I how we ended up with kids who love Jesus when so many pastors' kids rebel or become disillusioned with the church. Sure, there were a lot of good, intentional things we did along the way. We also screwed up a lot. But I'm convinced that the best thing we did for our kids was pray.

We prayed specifically and earnestly that our kids would love Jesus. It's no accident.

We also prayed for our girls' future husbands from the time they were little. Both of my sons-in-law became Christians when they were older. Coincidence? Maybe. Or maybe it was prayer. They didn't have Jesus when I was praying for them. I didn't even know who they were – one of them lived in England!

I love this verse from Ezekiel. God says, *I will give you a new heart and put a new spirit in you; I will remove from you your heart of stone and give you a heart of flesh* (Ezekiel 36:26 NIV). God is the only one capable of breaking through a heart that's hard—and he IS capable of it. I know there is at least one person on your mind who makes you think, "Man, that is a heart of stone if ever I've seen one! It would take a serious miracle for that person to become a Christian."

God can do it. Pray.

TIMING THE HARVEST

Here's the thing, though—some hearts take a long time to thaw. We talked about spiritual growth being a marathon and not a sprint, and the same can be said of your prayer life. Gene Appel, Senior Pastor of Eastside Christian Church, shared this story about a gold-medal marathon prayer warrior:

> *Recently a buddy of mine told me that his mother prayed every day for 40 years for his dad to become a follower of Jesus. She just kept praying and kept praying. She prayed year 1, year 5, year 10, year 20, year 30, kept praying. Finally, after 40 years, he became a follower of Jesus and decided he wanted to be baptized in the Jordan River in Israel. I mean, it was a dramatic conversion. As he told me the story, I thought, "What if she stopped praying after 39 years? What if she stopped after 39 years and just said, "You know, I don't think it's ever going to happen." Don't ever underestimate the power of your prayers for someone who has yet to experience the amazing grace of Jesus Christ.*

Can you imagine praying forty years for someone's salvation? That is serious commitment! It must be incredibly discouraging to see no results after so many years of patient investment. I have a feeling though, that if any of us had the opportunity to meet this woman, she would probably say she had no other choice. She obviously loved her husband deeply—she had to believe on his behalf. She couldn't give up on him.

Earlier in the book, I shared the story about how my son-in-law became a Christian through the work of a campus ministry in England. Well, Ash works for Dave Ramsey's company in Nashville, and I visited recently to do a devotional for all the staff. I shared Ash's story during that devotion—most of his co-workers had never heard it.

Later, Ash was talking with a co-worker who had some questions about his story. What university did he attend? What was the name of the campus ministry? The answers blew her away. As it turns out, this colleague used to work for Christian Missionary Fellowship, the parent organization of this campus ministry, and several years ago she had prayed for some random British guy named Ash to become a Christian! She had no idea that Ash actually had become a Christian, let alone married an American, moved to Nashville, and started working for the same Christian company.

This co-worker told Ash she had been feeling discouraged lately about the power of prayer and whether our prayers make any difference.

Incredible.

Let's return to Jesus' harvest analogy. I shared the first part of this passage early on, but there's more that we need to examine together.

"Don't you have a saying, 'It's still four months until harvest'? I tell you, open your eyes and look at the fields! They are ripe for harvest. Even now the one who reaps draws a wage and harvests a crop for eternal life, so that **the sower and the reaper may be glad together**. *Thus the saying 'One sows and another reaps' is true. I sent you to reap what you have not worked for. Others have done the hard work, and you have reaped the benefits of their labor"* (John 4:35-38 NIV, emphasis mine).

"One sows and another reaps." "I sent you to reap what you have not worked for." What does this mean?

Here, Jesus is speaking to the disciples, who we know will be crucial to the spreading of the gospel after Jesus' ascension into heaven. We know that when Peter gets up to preach his first sermon, three thousand people get on board. But it isn't just the work of these ex-fishermen that turns hearts to Jesus. For centuries, God's prophets readied the Jewish people for this Messiah. John the Baptist preached repentance and prepared people to encounter Jesus. Others had sown seeds along the way, and now it was time for the disciples to reap.

When your mission is to invest in lives, sometimes you'll get to reap . . . and sometimes you'll just be sowing seeds.

Sometimes you will pour your heart and soul into sharing God's love with a person, and you won't see them come to Christ. You might invest years, time spent serving, listening, loving, and praying, and never see any fruit.

Do it anyway.

Only God changes hearts. The timing of the harvesting process isn't up to us. Sometimes we reap, and sometimes we sow. And the thing is, you never know what might come of your efforts down the road. The woman you befriended who moved away might experience a crisis, think of something you said once, and step inside the doors of a church. That estranged family member with whom you tried to reconcile might meet a Christian co-worker who is able to lead him to Christ.

Someday, the sower and the reaper will be glad together, because we'll all be in heaven celebrating these amazing stories! We'll find out how our stories are intertwined, and it won't matter who did what, because we'll just be thrilled that people are there with Jesus.

Don't stop investing. Your mission isn't to manipulate hearts— your mission is to connect, serve, share, grow, and pray. The rest is up to God.

PRAYER CHANGES OUR FOCUS
One other crucial reason we pray for the people we're hoping to reach is that we need God to fix our vision. We slide so easily from grace into judgment, from proclaiming Jesus to having a savior

complex. There is no room for pretension in this mission—Jesus made that pretty darn clear.

"Do not judge, or you too will be judged. For in the same way you judge others, you will be judged, and with the measure you use, it will be measured to you.

"Why do you look at the speck of sawdust in your brother's eye and pay no attention to the plank in your own eye? How can you say to your brother, 'Let me take the speck out of your eye,' when all the time there is a plank in your own eye? You hypocrite, first take the plank out of your own eye, and then you will see clearly to remove the speck from your brother's eye" (Matthew 7:1-5 NIV).

How do we avoid being the idiot with the plank-eye? We pray. We go to God and remember that he's big and we're small. We go to the cross and remember that we're all failures who put Jesus there, but that his sacrifice is big enough to cover everything. It's impossible to have a savior complex at the foot of the cross.

And something amazing happens when we pray in earnest for people. We actually start to love them more.

When you spend time talking to God about a friend, you can't help but see that friend as a person for whom Jesus died. You know God is just waiting to run to this prodigal, throw an Armani jacket on his shoulders and tell him he's home.

Talk to God. He wants his kids home even more than you do.

CHAPTER 18

SUIT UP

"GOD DESIGNED IT THIS WAY; HE INTENDED THAT HIS GREAT POWER, WISDOM, AND LOVE SHOULD BECOME VISIBLE IN VERY ORDINARY AND OTHERWISE INCONSEQUENTIAL PEOPLE."

- RAY C. STEDMAN

On March 28, 1990, in a game against the Cleveland Cavaliers, Michael Jordan of the Chicago Bulls scored a career high 69 points. (This was just a couple of months after Denise and I moved to Chicago . . . I admit, it was a decent consolation prize to finally get to root for a great team.) In that same game, Stacy King, in one of his first games with the Bulls, was on the court for 17 minutes, missed four shots from the field, and made one of two free throws for a grand total of one point. A few days later in a newspaper interview, a reporter asked Stacy what was his greatest memory so far as a player in the NBA. He didn't even have to think: "I'll never forget that night Michael Jordan and I together scored 70 points in a single game!"

This is it, folks. This is how we win the game. This is how we accomplish our mission. This is what you need most as you lay down this book and walk out into the world. It's prayer—specifically, the prayer that unlocks the power of the Holy Spirit in your life.

Other people might see 70 points on the scoreboard. God can and wants to do immeasurably more in our lives than we could ask or imagine. But we know the reality of the situation—it's 69 points for the Holy Spirit, and we earned our one point just by showing up on the court!

That was exactly how it happened for the early church.

But you will receive power when the Holy Spirit comes on you; and you will be my witnesses in Jerusalem, and in all Judea and Samaria, and to the ends of the earth (Acts 1:8 NIV).

Quite a tall order for such a ragtag group of followers. You have to remember exactly whom Jesus was talking to here. This was the same motley crew that had been following him for the last three years. Three years and they STILL couldn't get it right. Never once do you ever hear Jesus say to his disciples, *Man, you guys have such great faith, I am so proud of you!* Instead, over and over again, he had to say to them, *Don't you guys get it? How long have I been with you and you still have such little faith?*

And Jesus is going to hand the church and the future of Christianity over to these guys? Yes. Why? BECAUSE OF THE POWER. "You will receive power . . . " That's the secret. It was the power, not the people. He could have used anybody who was willing, and that's why he can use you and me because the same power is available to us today.

When you see a man or woman accomplishing great things for God, it is always the Holy Spirit working through them. When you hear stories about bold and selfless Christians around the world and think—"Wow, I could never do that!"—you're not wrong. Alone, you never could. But when the Holy Spirit is on your team, *nothing* is impossible.

STAYING CONNECTED

The key is the connection. Listen to Jesus' words to the disciples in John 15: *"I am the vine; you are the branches. If you remain in me and I in you, you will bear much fruit; apart from me you can do nothing. If you do not remain in me, you are like a branch that is thrown away and withers; such branches are picked up, thrown into the fire and burned. If you remain in me and my words remain in you, ask whatever you wish, and it will be done for you. This is to my Father's glory, that you bear much fruit, showing yourselves to be my disciples"* (John 15:5-8 NIV).

How do you remain connected to the vine, connected to Jesus? Prayer! And this isn't just the "God is great, God is good" mealtime kind of prayer. It's not confined to early-morning quiet times or church services. This is prayer from the trenches.

This is relying on God on a moment-by-moment basis.

In Paul's letter to the Thessalonian church, he tells them to "pray continually" (1 Thessalonians 5:17). That kind of prayer is a habit. Do you know anyone with an incredibly annoying habit like pencil-tapping or knuckle-cracking? (With your luck, it was probably the guy sitting next to you in the meeting this morning.) People do that sort of thing without even thinking about it. They do it all day long. They fall into the activity seemingly without any sort of conscious thought.

That should be us, talking to God! Prayer should be our go-to. Our gut reaction. Our dialogue with God should be ongoing, like a text conversation that never ends. You've gotten some unexpectedly good news? You're celebrating with God. You're enjoying a beautiful sunset on your drive home? You're thanking God. You're worried about your friend in the hospital? You're pouring your worries out to God. You're about to give a presentation that makes you nervous? You're asking God for peace and courage.

In fact, James said something remarkably similar: *Is anyone among you in trouble? Let them pray. Is anyone happy? Let them sing songs of praise. Is anyone among you sick? Let them call the elders of the church to pray over them and anoint them with oil in the name of the Lord* (James 5:13-14 NIV).

Make prayer a habit! Stay connected to your power source.

Of course, a dialogue implies that the communication goes both ways, doesn't it? It's as much listening as it is talking. You can't get your orders from God if you're not praying. What if God wants you to go talk to someone or show someone some compassion? How is he going to let you know that if you're not in constant communication with him? What if someone you're talking to is ready right now to receive Christ? How will you know that? Are you going to force God to drop an anvil on your head every time he wants your attention? I don't think that's the kind of relationship he wants; nor do you. Prayer is the way he leads us. The more you are in prayer, the more you can sense that gentle tug of the Holy Spirit to do this or that. It might be God trying to tell you, "This is your point! Take the shot!"

If you find yourself going for days without remembering to stop and acknowledge God, let me help you out. I realize that praying continually doesn't always come naturally to us self-absorbed humans, and Satan is going to try to do everything he possibly can to distract you from prayer. So if this is you, if you've let clutter get in the way of your dialogue, here are some ideas to establish the habit.

Try driving in silence. Shut the radio off for awhile. Use your commute to talk to God—and listen.

Get an app. There are a ton of Bible apps out there, get one that sends you a verse every day. Who doesn't need to be interrupted by truth?

Put some Post-Its® up on your mirror, your dash, your front door.

Put a reminder on your phone or computer. Seriously. Create a reminder that pops up every single hour. We check our text and email alerts religiously, don't we? That habit already exists. Set yourself a reminder to stop throughout the day and continue your conversation with God.

I want to challenge you to do it at 10:02 every day. Stop—set your alarm right now. AM or PM—or both, I don't care. Luke 10:02 (NIV) is the verse that says, *"The harvest is plentiful, but the workers are few. Ask the Lord of the harvest, therefore, to send out workers into his harvest field."*

So set it for 10:02.

These ideas might seem kind of trite to you, but I am telling you—you can either let technology be a curse and a distraction or you can claim it for your spiritual life. God can use anything. It takes time to create a new habit, and this is a habit worth owning. Do *whatever it takes* to make prayer second nature.

You can't survive without it.

SUIT UP

Listen to this story that Dave Stone, pastor of Southeast Christian Church in Louisville, shared with me recently:

> *Several months ago, I was talking with a man who's a missionary in a primarily Muslim culture. He has been beaten. He has been stoned. He's had people come to his home. He actually has a hidden tunnel underneath his house. He has guard dogs trying to protect him because there are so many people that want to take his life. He got talking to me about how he prays for a couple of hours every morning. I asked him, "Would you ever think about entering your day without praying first?" He gave me a look like I was from another planet. He said, "Not to pray would be suicide."*
>
> *He got me to thinking. In our American culture, we're a long ways from that . . . at least I am personally. I found that when I pray, "coincidences" happen. When I don't pray, they don't happen. I'm better off when I invite God into my day and say, "Lord, will you lead me to the people you want me to visit with today, will you find someone for me to encourage? Is there someone that I can pray with? Is there something that I can do on your behalf?" When I begin my day with prayer, it's as if he dictates my decisions and directs my steps. When I don't, I feel like I spin my wheels.*

Not to pray would be suicide.

We are in a battle—a spiritual war—but unless you know how to access your spiritual resources through prayer, you cannot know spiritual victory. And God has called you and me to victory. He has called us to be the ones—the ones through whom he demonstrates his power from heaven to earth to show everyone, everywhere, that what he is accomplishing is greater than whatever this world throws at us, today.

You are the one . . . I am the one.

And Satan is also behind the scenes battling for the souls of as many people as he can pull away from God. He has one goal, and that is destruction. He's no idiot. He knows he's already lost, but he's going to try and take as many people down with him as he possibly can. That's why your mission and mine is so important. The fight is over the souls of men and women — your friends and mine, your relatives and mine. We cannot fight this battle alone, but that's really the good news, because we don't have to. Our battle belongs to the Lord.

It's time to suit up.

Finally, be strong in the Lord and in his mighty power. Put on the full armor of God, so that you can take your stand against the devil's schemes. For our struggle is not against flesh and blood, but against the rulers, against the authorities, against the powers of this dark world and against the spiritual forces of evil in the heavenly realms. Therefore put on the full armor of God, so that when the day of evil comes, you may be able to stand your ground, and after you have done everything, to stand. Stand firm then, with the belt of truth buckled around your waist, with the breastplate of righteousness in place, and with your feet fitted with the readiness that comes from the gospel of peace. In addition to all this, take up the shield of faith, with which you can extinguish all the flaming arrows of the evil one. Take the helmet of salvation and the sword of the Spirit, which is the word of God.

Here's our reference to that ongoing dialogue:

And pray in the Spirit on all occasions with all kinds of prayers and requests. With this in mind, be alert and always keep on praying for all the Lord's people. (And this last part is Paul's request for himself that we can interpret today as what we need to be praying for each other.) *Pray also for me, that whenever I speak, words may be given me so that I will fearlessly make known the mystery of the gospel, for which I am an ambassador in chains. Pray that I may declare it fearlessly, as I should* (Ephesians 6:10-20 NIV).

I want that power, don't you? I want to be equipped for this mission. I don't want my life to be explainable without the power of the Holy Spirit.

I want the Good News about Jesus to completely rock my Jerusalem the way it did in the early church. I want to see lives transformed, shook up, turned upside-down. I want to see heaven on earth…and when I get to heaven someday, I want to see a lot more of earth in heaven.

But you will receive power when the Holy Spirit comes on you; and you will be my witnesses in Jerusalem, and in all Judea and Samaria, and to the ends of the earth.

This is your mission . . . should you choose to accept it.

Are you ready?

ENDNOTES

Introduction
1. Courtesy of Rick Rusaw, Pastor of LifeBridge Church.
2. Keep Believing Ministries: Equipping and Encouraging People to Keep Believing in Jesus.

Chapter 2
3. Wayne Cordeiro, North American Christian Convention.
4. Kolenda, Daniel. ""God's Relentless Love"" Danielkolenda.com: A Blog for Evangelists (blog), March 8, 2010. Accessed May 22, 2014. http://danielkolenda.com/2010/03/08/godsrelentlesslove/.

Chapter 3
5. Lewis, C. S. *The Problem of Pain*. New York, NY: HarperOne, 2001.
6. Strobel, Lee. *The Case for Faith*. Grand Rapids, MI: Zondervan, 2002.
7. Lewis, C. S. *The Great Divorce*. New York: Macmillan, 1946.
8. Willard, Dallas. Apprentice Institute (formerly spelled Aprentis) Conference 2011: "The Ingredients of Transformation into Christlikeness: Vision, Intention, and Means." Wichita, KS. Aprentis Institute.

Chapter 6
9. Mehta, Hemant. *I Sold My Soul on EBay: Viewing Faith through An Atheist's Eyes*. Colorado Springs, CO: Waterbrook, 2007.
10. "A New Generation Expresses Its Skepticism and Frustration with Christianity." Barna. org. September 24, 2007. Accessed May 22, 2014. https://www.barna.org/barna-update/teens-nextgen/94-a-new-generation-expresses-its-skepticism-and-frustration-with-christianity#.U34yr15J-Ex.

Chapter 7
11. Sherrill, Elizabeth. "The Skunk." Evelyn's Wildlife Refuge Critter Tales 5 (December 2010): 2.

Chapter 8
12. Darley, John M., and C. Daniel Batson. ""From Jerusalem to Jericho": A Study of Situational and Dispositional Variables in Helping Behavior." Journal of Personality and Social Psychology 27, no. 1 (1973): 100-08. doi:10.1037/h0034449.

Chapter 9
13. Macleod, Scott. "The Life and Death of Kevin Carter." Time, September 12, 1994. Accessed May 22, 2014. http://content.time.com/time/magazine/article/0,9171,981431,00.html.
14. Shaw, Anup. "Today, around 21,000 Children Died around the World." - Global Issues. September 24, 2011. Accessed May 20, 2014. http://www.globalissues.org/article/715/today-21000-children-died-around-the-world.

Chapter 11

15. Clint Kelly. "Eugene Peterson: The Story Behind The Message". Lifeway.
16. Peterson, Eugene H. *Christ Plays in Ten Thousand Places: A Conversation in Spiritual Theology*. Grand Rapids, MI: W.B. Eerdmans, 2005.
17. Courtesy of Alan Hirsch.

Chapter 12

18. Parrott, Les, and Leslie Parrott. "The One Minute Marriage? - Drs. Les and Leslie Parrott." Drs Les and Leslie Parrott. Accessed May 22, 2014. http://www.lesandleslie.com/devotions/the-one-minute-marriage/.
19. Caroselli, Marlene. *Leadership Skills for Managers*. New York: McGraw-Hill, 2000.
20. Zacharias, Ravi K. *Jesus Among Other Gods: The Absolute Claims of the Christian Message*. Nashville, TN: Word Pub., 2000.
21. Bono, and Michka Assayas. *Bono*. New York: Riverhead Books, 2005.
22. Young, William P. *The Shack: A Novel*. Newbury Park, CA: Windblown Media, 2007.

Chapter 13

23. Coleman, Robert Emerson. *The Master Plan of Evangelism*. Westwood, NJ: F.H. Revell, 1964.

Chapter 14

24. Russell, Bob. *When God Builds a Church: 10 Principles for Growing a Dynamic Church: The Remarkable Story of Southeast Christian Church*. West Monroe, LA: Howard Pub., 2000.
25. Chandler, Matt. *To Live Is Christ to Die Is Gain*. S.l.: David C Cook, 2014

Chapter 15

26. Willard, Dallas. *Living in Christ's Presence: Final Words on Heaven and the Kingdom of God*.
27. Thomas, Gary. *Sacred Pathways: Discover Your Soul's Path to God*. Grand Rapids, MI: Zondervan, 2000.
28. *The Karate Kid*. Directed by John G. Avildsen and Robert M. Kamen. Performed by Ralph Macchio, Elizabeth Shue, Pat Morita. 1984. DVD.

ACKNOWLEDGMENTS

I'm so thankful for the people who helped make this book a reality. The big step was at some restaurant in Rwanda when Rick Warren said he wanted to get behind it. I'll admit, I didn't even have to pray about that one! To Josh Warren, Nadim, Kyle, and the team at Pastors.com—this is *our* project, and I'm so grateful to be in partnership with you. To John, thank you for your brilliant crafting. The Saddleback team is amazing—thank you Tom, Dave, Cody, Anne, and everyone for your support.

To my daughter, Rachel, my editor and re-write specialist, I would have had a nervous breakdown without you. Thank you for helping me, and for making me a grandchild.

To my family, I love you all. Thank you, Ash, for your help on the web and your support. Lauren and Tommy—for the edits and the love and the support. I'm so proud of your ministry. Becca—you are the example of this book in every way. My family lives this mission with me.

To my parents, Dan and Faye, who lived this mission first and gave it birth in me. To my in-laws, Don and Carol, who modeled it for my wife and are my biggest encouragers. To my sister Dana, and Jay—I love the way you live this.

There is a staff full of people who work with me at Parkview that I can't live without—especially my right arm, Bill, and my left arm, Jenny. Chaz, Casey, Karyn, Seth, Ricci, Leslie, and Wayne—thank you for your support and work on this project.

To a group of Elders who have always supported me and let me make plenty of blunders leading a church on mission—but never without their wisdom and incredible guidance.

To the Lifetogether Team—Brett and Allen—this whole thing was really your idea. Thank you for making something from nothing.

I have a band of brothers who keep me together. They are my accountability partners and life partners in every way. Ben Cachiaras, Greg Nettle, and Eddie Lowen—we will walk this journey together. And my brothers-in-law—Jack and Doug—I'm so lucky to have you with me on this journey. So many others: Rick, Dave, Cal, Mike, preacher friends who keep me in this.

Mentors—not just my dad and father-in-law—but Uncle Roy Wheeler, Ben Merold, Don Wilson, Bob Russell, Alan Ahlgrim, Dick Alexander, and others who don't want to claim me.

Parkview—my petri dish for mission. Thank you for following a very inadequate shepherd and hardly complaining when I go after the lost sheep.

To all the girls I've loved before . . . oh wait.

This is the hardest part of the book. There are so many people who have influenced and encouraged me, and us, in this venture. Let me just thank all of you for being in my life. Let's fill heaven together.

Finally, saving the most important for last, I thank God for loving me and for blessing me beyond measure. I turn this book over to You, knowing that I've left it in the only hands that matter.